All You
Need

is a Good
Idea!

All You Need

is a Good Idea!

How to create marketing messages

that Actually Get Results

Jay H. Heyman

WILEY

John Wiley & Sons, Inc.

Published by John Wiley & Sons, Inc., Hoboken, New Jersey
Published simultaneously in Canada

For general information on our other products and services or for technical support, please contact our Customer Care Department within the United States at (800) 762-2974, outside the United States at (317) 572-3993 or fax (317) 572-4002.

Wiley also publishes its books in a variety of electronic formats. Some content that appears in print may not be available in electronic books. For more information about Wiley products, visit our web site at www.wiley.com.

Library of Congress Cataloging-in-Publication Data:

Heyman, Jay H. 1939-
    All you need is a good idea! : how to create marketing messages that actually get results / Jay H. Heyman.
        p.   cm.
    Includes bibliographical references and index.
    ISBN 978-0-470-23791-5 (cloth)
        1. Marketing.   2. Advertising.   3. Small business—Marketing.   I. Title.
    HF5415.H449 2008
    658.8—dc22

                                                                        2007052407

Printed in the United States of America

10 9 8 7 6 5 4 3 2 1

This book is to and for my wife Bonita.
Bonnie, read it, use it, enjoy it.

"Imagination is more important than knowledge."

—Albert Einstein

CONTENTS

THE BLANK PAGE

Before we officially get started, please allow me to introduce you to The Blank Page.

See it over there, opposite this page, staring wordlessly at you? It can be the most intimidating entity you will ever encounter. Everyone who writes, draws, paints, or in any way uses their creativity has to face it. So will you, if you believe in the inevitability of needing a powerful marketing insight, because what you will have to do is fill that blank page with a good idea. (It may not literally be a blank "page." It might be a storyboard, blog, podcast, sign, or brochure. But at the beginning, it is terrifyingly empty.)

Some business-related problem has brought you here. It is a lonely place to be. Right now you single-handedly have the responsibility to solve a creative challenge. There is a reasonable chance that you have no idea what to do next. It is not the problem of the person standing next to you, nor is it the problem of someone else in your organization. It is your mission, and you have either been forced or chosen to accept it. Until there is something on that page, it is not yet a group cooperative effort.

(Be assured that others will be around once the page is no longer blank. They will modify, change, improve, adjust, and make suggestions. Some will be excellent, some less so. Your response, if only to yourself, will be, "Thanks, but where were you when the page was blank?")

I can reassure you, however, that when you do create that good idea (you don't have to do it just yet, there are many chapters of direction, advice, and support coming up), there are few feelings that compare. It is unlike winning a trophy or getting a bonus; those are rewards others give to you. Creating the foundation of a good idea is a personal feeling of success and achievement. As you look at the idea you have created, it is energizing and revitalizing. You somehow just know that it is good and immediately understand how it will work in an ad, brochure, everywhere you need it. You feel proud, heading towards conceited, as you think, "Hey, there was nothing there before, and now look. I, me, myself created something."

You now have two choices. You can say, "Is the author kidding? Does he realize how completely 'skinny-dipping in the ole creek' naked that page over there is?" and then close this book and look at the next one on the shelf.

Or you can resolve to read this book and discover techniques you can use to create good ideas to fill that page and others like it.

One of those two choices is a good idea.

ACKNOWLEDGMENTS

Let me first thank all the clients, past and present, who allowed me to create marketing ideas for their companies. Without their trust, this would be a much shorter book.

Also, I am indebted to Shirley and Elliott Porte for entrusting us as the new stewards of their eponymous New Jersey advertising agency, allowing it to cross unaccompanied over the river and into New York.

Additionally, there are the numerous ad agency writers, art directors, producers, account executives, and top management from whom I learned so much. Some did it by demonstration; others stood as examples of what to avoid.

Then there is my family, constantly encouraging me to continue writing this book with observations such as, "It seems like forever, will you never find a publisher?" (Much thanks to Kathy Green, my agent, for putting an end to their skepticism. Along with Matt Holt and his marketing and PR team at John Wiley & Sons, Inc. for having faith that this book might actually be a good idea.)

My fellow BNI (a business networking organization) chapter members must be singled out for having endured more than most. They have gone from hearing me claim,

"I am writing a book," to hearing me whine that, "I am shopping my book around," to, finally, proudly, "I am having my book published." I kept several of them in mind as I wrote each section, making sure that each point would be as clear and as useful to a single proprietorship as to an employee of a larger corporation.

I believe I clearly remember the circumstances regarding the creation of each of the ideas in this book—I do not have the same degree of certainty as to what the weather was like last Tuesday. It is possible I have confused some specifics or omitted some credit. All was done to the best of my recollection; if your version of the truth differs meaningfully from mine, please let me know.

Finally, there is my agency co-founder and partner, Paul Mesches. Shortly after our wonderful and mutual friend Susan Fetto introduced us, I suggested to Paul that we should open our own ad agency. It made complete sense to me; we had no clients, no experience in running an agency, had never worked together, and had families to support. Perhaps that explains Paul's initial hesitation. After further discussions, he asked me the question we now have heard versions of from virtually every prospective client, "Suppose I were to say yes. What would be the next step?"

I thought about it briefly and gave the only honest answer I could, "What the hell do I know?" Somehow that seemed to give Paul the reassurance he needed.

Sixteen years later we are fortunate that we continue to look at most problems from entirely different perspectives. I say fortunately because we have discovered that, while we have very similar values, we have very different business skills. No surprise, given our dissimilar career paths and training. Happily this has made the division of labor—creative, strategic planning, traffic, production, media—almost intuitive. Of course we still try to pile as much as possible onto the other partner's plate. I may have been more successful in that regard, since Paul has gone from being a scratch golf player when we started to currently having a 12 handicap.

PREFACE

"I'm sayin' I don't know what to do."
"That's okay," he said. "That's how everything starts.
First you don't know an' then you do."
—Walter Mosley, *Fear of the Dark*

This book will show you how to develop good creative marketing ideas. Ideas that will help you stand out in the marketplace, build market share, and become a true brand with a unique identity. Ideas that will make your budget work harder than you ever thought possible. Ideas that will get you free publicity, enable you to look bigger than you really are, and get your competition nervous. All this can be accomplished without spending a fortune and while actually having fun. You'll discover the power of relevant shock and why lazy is good.

Good ideas build your business better and faster than ordinary ideas. Not a particularly shocking concept, but it is amazing how many companies and people settle for the ordinary and obvious, never having learned to recognize the difference between a good idea and a commonplace one. Or had the time or the ability to create a good idea.

Good ideas are not influenced by the size of your marketing budget. You don't settle for a weak idea with the justification that, after all, it's only going to be used for a single mailing. In fact, nothing can hurt the search for a good idea faster than the knowledge that it will be supported by a huge media budget. Because then the tendency is to go for the safe idea, not the unusual one, hoping that the many consumer exposures will make up for the flatness of the message. After reading this book, you should feel confident that you understand how to develop good ideas that will build your business. You will discover innovative ways to expand the uses for ideas you already have. You will certainly gain a better understanding of how to judge ideas that others bring to you.

At the very least, if you develop just one good idea or learn how to tweak a weak idea and shape it into a better one, I suggest that is well worth the time you spend reading this book. Certainly it is worth whatever the cost of the book itself might be. In fact, I wanted to offer you a money back guarantee. However, the book's title not withstanding, my publisher didn't think that would be a good idea.

By The Way:
1. I use the word "Phufkel" to stand for your product or service. Even if you don't make or sell Phufkels, think of it as representing whatever it is you do for a living. (And if you do actually manufacture Phufkels, I could use some more, in green.)
2. This book is written in plain, straightforward, clear, conversational English. (Though wherever possible, grammatically correct.) As in much of life, there are two reasons:

    First, too much fancy argot can get in the way. You don't need me to tell you about ROI, BDI, streams of revenue, or my personal favorite,

EBITDA (earnings before interest, taxes, deprecia-
tion and amortization).

Secondly, well, it's just the way I tend to write.
Having spent a career lifetime writing commercials and ads, I quickly discovered that ten-dollar
words just got in the way. When you only have
about 60 of them in a 30-second commercial, you
have to make each word count and be clear, or
you will immediately lose your audience as they
scurry to a dictionary, or more likely, head for the
kitchen. I will, however, throw in some really nice
long words once in a while, just to show I can.

INTRODUCTION

During my career in advertising, I've created campaigns for corporations and products such as Procter & Gamble, General Mills, Ralston Purina, and Skippy peanut butter. Everything from television campaigns for the nation's largest advertisers to tabletop signs for a local restaurant. I've been honored with awards, plaques, and trophies. Some of my commercials are in the Paley Center for Media—formerly the Museum of Television and Radio—in New York.

For the past 16 years, as co-founder, creative director and president of my own New York ad agency, I've also created marketing pieces for smaller companies. I've learned that every client—no matter the size—has the same need for powerful creative marketing ideas.

The difference is that smaller businesses like yours—and according to the Small Business Administration, small businesses account for more than 90 percent of all businesses in the United States, so you're not alone—don't always have the resources and large staff to develop these ideas. Or have the budget to hire an ad agency. Working with a good ad agency—and with the good ones it is always working *with*—can help you create ideas more quickly, with results that you often could never come up with on your own. (After you read this book, can you imagine the thrilled expression on your advertising agency's face when you knowledgeably critique the creative material it presents to you or ask to see the strategy it worked with? Even better, can you imagine the look of unquestionable pleasure on their faces when you actually present *your* ideas to *them?*)

This book contains some of the principles I've discovered, modified, and simplified. You'll find that incorporating these principles into your business philosophy will take the mystery out of using marketing creativity to build your business.

All You Need Is A Good Idea! is intended to educate, coach, and instruct in an informal, casual manner. It is not a lecture; it is a discussion designed to get you involved. Every chapter includes three elements: First, a vital component of the idea process is presented. These facilitate the development of creating good ideas, provide an understanding of why that part of the process is necessary, and what can be accomplished. Next comes a case history of a marketing effort I was personally involved with that will further illustrate the point covered in the chapter. Finally, each chapter will have at least one "Good Idea" portion, offering specific suggestions on how to think about relating the example being used to the creation of a marketing idea for your own business.

Throughout the book, you will see firsthand how I went about developing ideas for, among other companies, Frigidaire, Rapid Park garages, the Stage Deli, and the American Arbitration Association. I also have included some case histories that, though wonderful examples of good ideas and helpful in illustrating a creative point, for various reasons never saw the light of an ad page or glow of a television set. (Anacin and Vaseline Petroleum Jelly come sorrowfully to mind.)

While the creative portion is just one part of the total marketing mix, it is often the most difficult to master. After you establish your business based on your product or service, (for our purpose we will refer to this as a Phufkel) you have all the traditional elements of marketing to consider, such as pricing, research, media selection, and channels of distribution.

Pick the wrong price point? Painful!

Misinterpret your research? Ouch!

But I submit to you that the most important part of your marketing is generating the idea. Get that part wrong or get it bland and you will suffer the death of a thousand silent cash registers.

There is a quotation from Albert Einstein in the front of the book. While I could not begin to explain his theory of relativity, I think I understand his assertion that "Imagination is more important than knowledge," at least when used in a marketing context. If you give a group of equally intelligent business people the same inputs, they will likely end up with the same conclusions. For example, provide a group of experienced media buyers the same marketing goal using traditional media such as radio, television, or newspapers, along with matching reach and frequency information, and if they are working strictly from the numbers, you will get back virtually identical media plans. But add in opportunities for creativity and imagination and the results will differ widely. As Chuck Brymer, president and chief executive at DDB Worldwide, said at a recent management conference of the American Association of Advertising Agencies and quoted in the *New York Times*, "Data is no substitute for creativity."

Additionally, you can only have knowledge of a finite number of facts. There is always going to be more information out there than you can put your hands on, Google or no Google, Wikipedia or no Wikipedia. But your creativity is only limited by your imagination. It is your imagination that will lead you to your good ideas, as you find new ways to tell people why your Phufkel is better, different, less expensive, improved, revolutionary, whatever.

Customers will only beat a path to your better Phufkel if they have actually heard about it. Creating a successful business requires harnessing the power of the unexpected idea, the relevant shock of unfamiliarity to stand out, and to get your message seen and then acted upon. Fortunately there is now a book—heck, you're holding it—that will help you create the good ideas you need.

Aside from a few instances used to illustrate a point, the examples I use in this book are for ideas—good ideas, not-as-good ideas, or the occasionally ordinary ideas— that I personally created. As the saying goes, "Been there. Done that." Of course, at the larger ad agencies, there are always others involved in the creative process: art directors, writers, creative directors, department heads, clients, account executives, top management. They could/would suggest changes, modifications, or improvements on the original idea. Depending upon how high up the food chain they were, or how good their input actually was, their ideas would be accommodated. But in the beginning of the process there is always just one person who comes up with the idea—one person and a blank page.

Phil Rosenthal, creator of the *Everybody Loves Raymond* television show, has this observation: "I don't know what a good idea is. Whose criteria is it? My idea of a good idea, or your idea of a good idea?" Like most creative endeavors—books, plays, paintings, sculpture, music— ideas are subjective, opinions varied, judgments diverse. You may not even agree that my tie goes with my jacket and shirt. (You would not be alone in this.)

Do not feel you have to follow each suggestion exactly, nodding your head in agreement with each example. Even when working with the same product, marketing information, and strategy, every art director I've ever worked with has come up with a visual solution that was different than any other art director developed. Every writer comes up with a different combination of words for body copy, a headline, or a slogan. You will have to bring your own sensibility, talent, and personality into the creation of your ideas. You may not always agree that every example I present is what you would consider a good idea. I do hope that, while we will not have absolute agreement, you find genuine inspiration in these pages, treating it as a collection of candid advice from someone who honestly wants to help you to do a better job of creating profitable marketing ideas.

Good Idea: Let's assume you are not entirely new to this. Many of you have taken at least a step in the direction of generating ideas and have produced some marketing pieces, either by yourself or with professional help. What I would like you to do, if you have an ad, a brochure, a sign, a press release, a storyboard, is to take it out and keep it next to this book. As you read along, glance over at your "piece." See if it truly accomplishes what you are learning you should want it to. See if you understand how to improve it or decide if you should start anew.

You are about to tell me that you don't have a brochure. But you do have a heck of a website. Also, what about your podcasts, blogs, RSS feeds? What about them? Sure they are modern technological communication wonders, but they are just the mechanics, the delivery systems.

If you have gone to a meeting at your office or as a committee member of some local group you belong to, at some point it is decided to create some marketing, maybe to get new members or perhaps to generate excitement for a fundraiser. One person immediately says, "Great, we need" — and then proudly lists, as if he were creating something insightful—"a newsletter, or a brochure, maybe a CD to send out, or perhaps an ad, some public relations . . ." He does not mean the list in the sense of let us not forget any of these possibilities. He truly means the list as the answer to the problem; once we have it, we are ready to go. The point again is that these are just the "things." Of and by themselves they have no value until they are filled with good ideas to make them effective. They are no different in terms of what you should be trying to accomplish with an idea than if your message was going to be placed on a matchbook cover or on a phone kiosk. The need to create good ideas is independent of the newest technology in communication. In fact, it might be just the opposite; new methods of communicating a marketing message will rely even more heavily on the power to create a good idea to differentiate the company or product. After all, when everyone you know is writing blogs (70,000 new blogs a day, according to Technorati.com), what does it take to make a particular blog stand out? What's that you say? A good idea can make a blog stand out? Interesting, I never thought of that.

It is my goal to help you stand out from your competition by actually having people notice your marketing communications. Instead of relying on clichéd messages that no one really sees, you will learn how to determine what is unique about your business and how to communicate that difference in a surprising, compelling manner. You will begin to include at least a dollop of the unexpected in every communication, from your brochures and signage to your commercials, website, and direct marketing programs.

This book will guide you in the rewarding (both financial and artistic) discovery of how essential good ideas are, along with the steps necessary to create them. Since nothing will hinder the development of a good idea faster than a tense atmosphere, a stern judge, and overly demanding instructor, my intention is to have as much fun as you will during the process.

ABOUT THE TITLE

This book is called *All You Need Is A **Good** Idea*. It is not titled *All You Need Is A **Great** Idea*. While you are waiting for the "world's greatest" idea you will stand frozen in fear, immobilized by anxiety. You will find yourself conscientiously discarding all the ideas you create, judging them as not being good enough, or a little trite, or not quite clever enough. You will never satisfy yourself sufficiently to actually use one of them.

There is a saying that "Perfect is the enemy of good." If you keep prodding, tweaking, and tampering with something good, trying to turn it into something perfect, you will not just miss a lot of important deadlines. It is possible you might never get there at all, in effect turning a good idea into no idea.

Why settle for just "good" ideas, you ask. Shouldn't you always swing for the bleachers, aim for the stars and all that good guidance your teachers and coaches have always motivated you with? Sure you should. But let's get real. If your field were music, would the realization that you would never be as great as Mozart stop you from starting? Not being Shakespeare has not prevented other writers from getting tons of books published, read, and enjoyed. A few were great, many were good, which is the point. Do good, even if you can't do great. It is not compromising. It is simply more realistic.

The practical point is that I don't want you to stand motionless at a creative standstill caused by the worry that your idea isn't brilliant enough. I want you to avoid waiting for that explosion of inspiration, that unbelievably perfect miraculous idea that will cause long lines to form. It is more practical, and in the long run more helpful, to come up with a good idea than to come up with no idea at all. It doesn't mean that you are settling for less than the best. The constant use of good ideas will get you/your Phufkel/your business more attention than the elusive blockbuster idea that comes along about as often as a Bill Bernbach or David Ogilvy. (No, you probably don't know them.)

Words and ideas that are fresh and unexpected will jump off the page, do handsprings, whistle off-key, anything it takes to grab attention and shout, "Look at me. Look at me!" On the other hand, there are some thoughts that are so worn-out you will never even notice their presence, such as "On the other hand." It is the difference between the life of the party and the wallflower. Both may be perfectly wonderful people, but no one goes home from the event chatting about the guy in the corner who kept looking at his shoes and not making eye contact. The last thing you want is a message that no one notices.

There are a fair number of these clichés available, but I suggest there is one that is the worst offender of all, because it usually seems so true and accurate as a reflection of your business: "LOW PRICES. GREAT SERVICE."

That's you, isn't it? That's what you really offer and deliver! I personally believe you. However, do you really think those words should be the center of a good marketing idea? The premise may be fine as a strategy, but please, never, never use them unadorned. Do you really think you will be able to capture people's attention, or their wallets, with words like that? Or ideas like:

- ◆ Taste is everything.
- ◆ No ___. No ___. No Kidding! (As in: No Banners. No Pop-ups. No Kidding. Or, No fees. No minimums. No kidding!)

- Deliciously Different.
- We'll match any price.
- You owe it to yourself to try it.
- Tomorrow's solutions. Today.
- Taste is always in season.
- Even when you can afford the best it's always nice to find excellence at a reduced price. (Yes, I have actually seen this headline.)
- Seeing is believing.
- Often imitated. Never duplicated.
- Money Talks. Nobody Walks. (You would never, would you?)

A good idea is so much better than a poor idea. And even a weak idea has it all over no idea at all.

What is the difference between a weak idea, a good idea, a great idea, and, heaven forbid, no idea at all?

WEAK IDEA

Weak ideas, like the preceding examples, will immediately sound familiar to you as you are creating them. That is one reason you can probably tell it is a weak idea. Without novelty or cleverness it will just sit there for you, as well as for whomever the message is intended. If, as you think about the idea you say to yourself, "I may have seen this somewhere before," then you probably have. While you may get credit for having a good memory, you get no praise for having found a good idea.

Sometimes a weak idea is not something you can immediately identify as familiar, but it is still a cliché and therefore invisible to the reader. For example, if you are launching or currently have a "light" version of your full-flavored, full-caloried Phufkel, you will probably put on your list of ideas, "The light at the end of the tunnel." You will start looking for a local tunnel to put the message on, because it seems like such a natural idea. Natural? Maybe. Good? Definitely not. Better than no idea at all? Barely.

GOOD IDEA

A good idea sounds fresh and new and presents itself in an arresting manner. It will slow down the audience, grab attention, and invite further inspection of your message. An unexpected splash of color, the precise word in a headline, a stopper of an illustration, a twist on your usual message, a new target, a different promise—anything can be part of the solution and help to turn a tired, weak idea into a good idea.

GREAT IDEA

A great idea is rare. It is something that can truly build your business single-handedly or solve a difficult marketing dilemma. There is an undeniable impact and power inherent in great marketing ideas. Think of Apple computers. I am not referring to the iconic introductory "1984" commercial, but to the marketing brilliance of the names themselves, "Macintosh" and "Apple." It was an invigorating approach that helped them immediately stand out from the competitions' computers with their gray boxes that used numbers for names and complex equations for keyboard commands. What a wonderful way to suggest the promise and benefits of an improved, friendlier user relationship.

Or consider the classic Absolut Vodka campaign. Again, I am not referring to the brilliance of the advertising itself, which focused on the bottle of Absolut. I am talking about the stream of innovative but relevant marketing promotion ideas: the bottle stockings, Father's Day silk ties, magnetic word puzzles, music chips—the list goes on and on.

As you watch TV, focus on the commercials. A few will be outstanding. Many you will consider an insult to your television; those are the ones that you will discover basically have no real idea to them. Either they are filled with clichés or are so hyped with production values that the visuals overpower any message that might have been present. But you will soon see what a good idea is and how it stands out from the majority of communications you watch. So good, in fact, you probably won't even zap right past it. Which is a good sign.

So go for the good.

CASE HISTORY: TOTAL CEREAL

Total is a breakfast cereal from General Mills. At the time I was working on it, the strategy was to convince adult consumers that it had more vitamins and minerals than other cereals, while still having great taste. The claim was that one serving of Total provided 100 percent of the minimum daily requirements of vitamins and iron. I created several ideas and, with the art director, John Sullivan, eventually presented them to the client. The commercial that was ultimately selected included the theme line, "Today is the first day of the rest of your life. Start it right with Total." Let me be very clear: I did not create the phrase "Today is the first day of the rest of your life." I leave the discovery of that phrase to William Safire. At the time it was on calendars, T-shirts, probably even inside fortune cookies. So I cannot take credit for the original thought.

What was a good idea was applying that thought— Today is the first day of the rest of your life—to a TV campaign for a breakfast cereal targeted not to kids, but to adults. We felt people would respond favorably to the message, because of, not in spite of, the familiarity of the theme. It was a good idea, though certainly not one that would forever revolutionize the breakfast cereal category. If I were looking for that revolutionary idea, I think I would still be sitting there, discarding that good idea and others just as good, waiting for the one ideal idea.

Good Idea: Is there a phrase that is current today that you could use as the basis for your own good idea? A phrase that is just "out there." The advantage is that everyone will immediately recognize it. The downside is that it may be unnoticed because it will seem too familiar and trite, thanks to overexposure. But, if you can figure out a middle ground, it could be a good start for your idea. Just as Taco Bell has done with "Think Outside The Bun," playing off "think outside the box" to suggest to customers they should avoid the clichéd habit of always eating a meal at the burger places. A little twist, a tweak, whatever it takes.

THE POWER OF AN IDEA

Welcome to the wonderful world of ideas.

You've been here before of course. Remember when you thought of putting cinnamon on top of your cola? Or when you decided to take digital photos of your old black and white family pictures, so that you would have them in a digital format without the expense and bother of scanning.

You've had product improvement ideas for your original Phufkel too, or ideas for a brand new Phufkel. You've had ideas on how to hold more productive sales meetings, grow a territory, shrink a budget, reward a key salesperson.

Very often you've seen the positive results. Good for you.

The world of the creative selling/marketing idea is even more rewarding.

More difficult? Sure. Possibly more fraught? No doubt. But there's nothing like the rewards you can achieve from a good idea.

As we all know, nothing is more powerful than an idea whose time has come, though I doubt Victor Hugo actually had this book in mind when he said that.

The question is this: Is it really worth the effort it can take to create a good idea? Do you really need one? Here's part of the answer: The market research firm Yankelovich, quoted in the *New York Times*, estimates "a person living in a city 30 years ago saw up to 2,000 ad messages a day, compared with up to 5,000 today." Given that information, we are left with the question, what does your business need to do to have your marketing message stand out from the other 4,999?

Perhaps the answer is simply to create a better Phufkel. But ask most businesses and they will tell you that often the problem is not creating the better mouse-trap. The problem is creating the marketing ideas that ensure their audience will find out about their mousetrap.

Maybe your answer is to dedicate a hefty advertising budget to your Phufkel. But too often a large budget means you may be tempted to settle for conservative and safe communications, in the hope that the weight of the media will help the message break through.

If the way to get your message heard is not a bigger marketing budget, then what is the answer? Let me build the tension and quote from Brian Steinberg's article in the Marketplace section of the *Wall Street Journal*."In the opening shot, a gleaming car hugs the curves of a sinuous road, the soaring Rockies filling the background. . . . Next, we see the once roaring auto at rest, basking in the sunshine. . . . Question: Is this an ad for: A) Ford, B) GM, C) Chrysler, D) Any of the above? If you picked D, you're right. For the most part, automobile commercials look alike. Most car ads are lame. They are boring," says Lance Jensen, chief executive at an independent ad firm. Adds Dave Sanabria, marketing communications manager for Ford Motor's Edge: "Let's face it. There is lots of advertising out there. You have to find ways to break through."

If automobile manufacturers, who throw millions and millions of dollars into marketing their products, realize it is not the budget but the need for breakthrough ideas, who am I to argue?

A good idea gives your company a unique and enduring identity. An idea can provide your company with positioning that helps you stand out in a notoriously crowded marketplace. It gets you noticed, shows people who you are, sells products, and builds market share. Good ideas are more than just slogans, more than a group of witty words nicely strung together. They are not cute and clever for the sake of being cute and clever. They have the strength to support a campaign and build a brand.

The powerful results of a good idea are obvious. Increased sales, phones ringing, toes tapping. (Yes, toes tapping. No joke. A good idea energizes you and your business: your presentations, your staff, your salespeople, your enthusiasm, your attitude.)

I don't know you personally. But I am willing to wager that you are not the only one who makes Phufkels. Someone else out there makes or sells Phufkels that are very similar to yours. Those people are called "the competition." And your competition is calling on, advertising to, visiting, and trying to sell to many of the people you are also contacting.

Now, you would love to sell more Phufkels than those other guys, wouldn't you? This is especially true if you once worked with them and most especially if you once worked *for* them. But how can you convince a prospect that your Phufkel is better/different? Or that your company is better/different? Look up your category (Phufkels) online or in the yellow pages. You might discover there are 5,430 Phufkel makers, 234 in your area alone!

Or there you are at the big trade show. Because of the system conference organizers use to set up these things, you are booth-to-booth with other Phufkel sellers, some with flashier displays, some with only one plain banner. The point is you are all selling Phufkels. Big or small, double coated or hi-tech. It is like olive oil at the NASFT Fancy Food Show at Javits Center in New York. Twelve booths feature cold-pressed olive oil. Eight display "virgin." Six booths sell "extra virgin." Then there are the purveyors of "single pressed." The promoters of "double pressed." It is confusing even to those who really know their oils. Similar products often make similar claims, using similar words and similar messages. So few businesses in any industry stand out. How can you?

Too often, unfortunately, most business owners haven't the foggiest idea.

But in a few more chapters you will. No, not the foggy ideas, the good ideas. Ideas that will help customers see your Phufkel from a new point of view and in a way they never thought of before.

Let me admit something: No one that I know has ever applauded a media plan. Granted, I may hang around with the wrong group of people. But there is something about an innovative selling idea that just makes smiles break out. As Peggy Noonan said in her Declarations column in the *Wall Street Journal*, "In modern life we wince a lot. It's not the worst thing, but it's better when something makes you smile."

A "smile" is a good test of an idea. Not particularly scientific, and if your business is running a funeral home perhaps it is not what you are really going for. For the most part, though, a smile often comes unbidden when a good idea appears on your computer, Post-it, or notepad. Part of the reason is that when you are finally in the zone and creating your ideas, sometimes you are writing them down so quickly you have to struggle to keep up with your thoughts. You have the feeling you are only taking dictation. Trust me, this experience does—and will—happen. But because you are not aware of laboriously trying to create the idea as you write it down, it is as if you are seeing it for the first time. So you look at it, and if it is good you smile. You do not smile because you have created it. You smile because, well, you just like the idea.

Here are some ideas that made me smile:

- One was reading about a Staples new product contest. The winner was someone who had the good idea of replacing the numbers on a combination lock with letters, so it could be set with an easy-to-remember word, rather than a series of numbers.
- Last week I received an outdoor rug I had ordered. When I opened up the cardboard box, inside was the folded rug, inserted inside a plastic zippered case. On one side of the plastic case there was a two-inch triangle, cut along two sides and held in place with Velcro. The good idea? On the lift-up triangle was printed the words: "Please Touch." The manufacturer wanted the purchaser to be able to feel how soft the material was to overcome resistance to purchasing a rug that sounded as if it would feel rough and harsh, since it was made from 100 percent polypropylene. What a nice change from all the "please don't touch" signs we see everywhere.
- Then there was the sign in the gift shop of the Museum of Jewish Heritage located in Battery Park City in New York. Not a particularly convenient location, especially if you are a tourist and have purchased a few gifts to bring back to your hotel or home. UPS, though, had a sign in the gift shop about a way to make the chore easier. It suggested, "Let us schlep your packages for you." Talk about targeting your audience.

♦ Recently, walking along Eighth Avenue in Manhattan. I noticed a double-decker tour bus filled with tourists. What made me smile was that it was not painted the traditional red, which, while indeed eye-catching, is the same color used by most of the city's bus operators. This bus was painted yellow and black to resemble a New York City taxi and indeed was called "New York Taxi Tours." Good idea. It cost them nothing (heck, they had to paint the bus some color anyway) while making them visually distinctive from their competition and more "New Yorky."

Good idea: Whether or not I specifically mention it every time, when I use an example of a good idea your brain should start clicking, thinking, and if the idea is serious enough, pondering. Can your business use an idea similar to what I am discussing? Would something comparable be effective for you?

"Hmmm, a yellow and black bus? I don't even own a bus. But wait, I do have a few trucks. Even have my company name on them. Maybe I should have more than just the address. Perhaps my company slogan. Or something eye catching. It is parked a lot and people would look at it. Perhaps a color. No, not pink, it is a plumbing repair company. But something. What do my competitors' trucks look like?" Why stop there? Maybe your business cards are due for a makeover. Your letterhead and what about . . .?

See where the power of a good idea can lead? It can do wonderful things for your business.

Here's a case history to demonstrate the power of a good idea. I will give you the punch line first: This idea never saw the light of day or the dark of night. It was simply never used. And while every creative person in advertising has a million stories of the campaigns that got away (bartender, another vodka martini, please), the point of including it is to help you understand the power of a good idea. You will recognize it as a good idea, and you will smile and get some insights from it. Or you will say, "He calls *that* a good idea?" and write your own book.

CASE HISTORY: SHARP WATCHES

Sharp watches was one of the accounts of an advertising agency I once worked for. The marketing strategy, as I recall, was intended to maintain and increase distribution, getting Sharp's revolving glass watch displays placed in as many outlets as possible. The creative strategy was to show a large variety of products. The 30-second television commercial I created was shot and put on the air. There were a variety of short shots of commonplace, boring objects, such as a glass globe with a painted rabbit in it, an exercise bike, a goldfish, a slice of white bread, a pocket protector, and a red brick. These were intercut (alternated) with close ups of various Sharp watches. As the objects were shown, the voice-over announcer (an announcer you hear, as distinct from an on-camera announcer, whom, as you might guess, is one you actually see) characterized the ordinary objects with the word "dull." Each time a watch was shown, he said "Sharp." So most of the copy went "Dull. Dull. Sharp. Dull. Sharp. Sharp." as the appropriate item was seen. Then came the tag line, created way before I got involved, "Sharp People Buy Sharp Watches."

It was pleasant enough, inexpensive to produce, and showed lots of product. But hopefully you realize that it should never be confused with something that you would rush home to tell your kids about, or delay going into the kitchen when it appeared on your television.

Then my good idea popped up, seemingly from nowhere. (When you least expect it and are thinking about something absolutely different or just drifting off to sleep, a solution often appears. Unless you have really good handwriting, be careful about writing down these ideas as you awake from your dream.) This was a completely different approach to the same product line. Sabino Caputo was the art director.

Picture a page in your favorite magazine. Printed on it are odds and ends of different pieces of paper torn from various sources and pasted on the page. All the scraps have one thing in common: They each contain the word "sharp." Not used as the name of the watch, but used as everyone does when they want to make sure people show up promptly at the proper time. One visual was of a yellow Post-it with "Call Donald about buying helicopter, yacht and casino. 3:30 **SHARP!**" written on it. Another scrap was of a page torn from a telephone pad. In the message area was this handwritten message: "Car pool will be at front door at 5:45 **SHARP!**" Next to that on the page was a torn piece of a white napkin with this scrawled on it: "Call Ron tonight at home 11:00 **SHARP!**" Another piece of the page design was part of a formal invitation, and the words you could see were ". . . you to attend"; ". . . vern on the green"; ". . . evening of October 3, 6:30 P.M. **SHARP**." There were one or two others on the page, including a copy of an ad for a theater listing that read, "Tomorrow's performance, at 8 P.M. **SHARP!**"

At the bottom of the ad was a picture of a watch, and whatever mandatory legal copy was needed. Centered among all the pieces of paper was the only text: "*Ever*

Notice That When People Are Serious about Time, They Always Mention Our Name?"

That is a good idea with the power of a good idea.

It is unexpected but relevant, will get readers nodding in agreement with the premise, has the possibility of a long useful life, and could not be used by others. ("Meet me tomorrow at 10:00 TIMEX!" doesn't work quite as well as "10:00 SHARP," does it?)

Good idea: Once you have your idea, think about what else you can do with it, as in "use the whole carcass," discussed in Chapter Twelve. Let's say you had come up with the "Ever notice . . ." idea for Sharp. Think about what else you could do with the idea. Not only for different versions of the print ad or the TV commercial. Think about other marketing opportunities. You could create phone message pads with the word "Sharp" already printed near the time field to help reinforce the name. Or distribute a brochure with the secrets of how to be punctual, sponsored by, who else . . .?

Why wasn't it ever used? Simple. The client had recently produced a commercial and had no need at that particular time to actually think about doing any new marketing. When I presented it again, the next time, it was old news. But we do know a good idea when we see one, don't we?

Dave Girouard, vice president and general manager of the Google software for businesses unit, said in the *Wall Street Journal,* "A lot of analytical stuff will give you incremental improvement, but it won't give you a big leap. You can't time or plan for innovation. It can't come from customer data. It has to come from the heart of somebody with an idea."

3

WHO DO YOU THINK YOU ARE, ANYWAY?

Please understand, I don't mean this question in a confrontational sense along the lines of "You are really loud-mouthed and arrogant. Why did you push ahead of me in line?" I mean it in the sense that the first thing you have to accomplish if you want customers to know who you are is for *you* to genuinely understand who you are. What is the essence of your business, the fundamental nature of your Phufkel? In short, what is your reason for being? What do you believe makes your Phufkels different? Why are yours better? While the answer to why you are selling your Phufkels should not simply be as glib as "to make money," neither should you spend too much time on the couch seeking faultless "I have journeyed to the mountain" answers. You probably already have some definitive ideas and an intuitive grasp of who you are, but it is essential that you write it down. Not as a mission statement. Not as a business plan. It is not a description of who you think your customer base is or a list of benefits of your Phufkels. It is, rather, a brief, basic summation of what your product or service is, to be used as a guide, a strategic direction for the marketing ideas you will be creating. There is an important reason for doing this, aside from the clarity it brings to your thinking. The really good marketing ideas—like the ones you will be creating—come directly out of your Phufkel and are not just layered on top of it.

If your Phufkel requires 17 steps to operate, you will have a difficult time convincing customers that the most important reason to buy your product is ease of operation, no matter how cleverly you make that claim. (Unless, of course, your competitors' Phufkels require 24 steps.) Keep in mind, however, that the knowledge of who you are is not what is going to differentiate you from your Phufkel competitors. Knowing who you are lets you understand *what* you want to communicate; it does not tell you *how* to communicate. That's where the idea part comes in.

It is like the definition I somehow still remember from a science class in PS 99 in Brooklyn. (Thank you, Mr. Datlof.) When you want to create a fire, you require certain things. Fuel, for example, is necessary, but it is not sufficient. You also need heat and oxygen. Well, when you want to create good ideas, knowing who you are is definitely required as a first step. But it is only the first necessary step on the path.

CASE HISTORY: PORTE ADVERTISING

This example may not be the most impressive brand name in the book, but it is one that will help you understand how to define your company, which is a really good idea. When Porte Advertising was created in 1993, my partner Paul Mesches and I had no real idea of what we had created, of who we were. We knew our different backgrounds and work histories—mostly at big ad agencies—our middle initials and our Social Security numbers. But what kind of company the agency was and how we were different from other advertising agencies was not something we immediately understood.

Naming the agency was the easy part. My wife Bonita's maiden name was Porte, but the agency was not named in a romantic tribute. The name had a far more practical application. My in-laws had started a printing company in New Jersey some 30 years earlier. They also had some advertising clients they serviced under the name Porte Advertising. They had kept a listing in the register of advertising agencies—The Red Book—listing some local accounts, active and less active. When we started our New York agency, we simply had business cards printed that said Porte Advertising with the New York address. (Did my in-laws approve? Heck, they printed the cards for us.) That really helped in meetings during the early days when the inevitable *Butch Cassidy and the Sundance Kid* question came up: Who are those guys? The answer was simply that we were the new management of Porte Advertising, the new New York branch. That gave us instant credentials and credibility, and the question went away, though there were lots of other questions to replace that one.

Good Idea: Are you a recent start-up? Do you need more credibility than you have? How about telling prospects about your business degrees or the groups, trade associations, and boards you belong to, or awards you have won? Is your previous track record impressive? Are there people in your company well known in your industry? Can you get testimonials from previous clients? Can you provide introductory pricing or on-time guarantees to get prospects to try you? Can you get speaking engagements in front of likely prospects?

What could Porte Advertising tell prospective clients besides the fact that we were the new management, the brash, eager, aggressive, talented new management? At first, we did what every small company does. We took the unavoidably obvious truth of our small size and made it a benefit, stating all the reasons why our modest size was good: no layers, you are dealing with the principals, quick turnaround, no wasted meetings, no politics, no costly overhead structure, we work more efficiently, more economically. In short, all the things you say if you are a small company. (This, of course, is merely the opposite of what you say to prospective clients when you are the big boy on the block: You claim depth of talent, it is easier to service clients, you can be reached at anytime, lots of services available, not stretched too thin.)

Our first brochure said that Porte Advertising was created out of the desire to provide creative, business-building communications on a cost-efficient basis. In hindsight that was like a chef trying to convince customers to order a hamburger by listing it on the menu as "cooked, chopped dead cow." It's accurate, but not particularly appealing.

As we evolved, we began to position ourselves as being able to make our clients look bigger, even with their smaller budgets. We said we were able to do this because of the constant attention we paid looking for unexpected ways to help them grow their business. We didn't simply ask for ever-increasing media budgets. And it was true. We did look for innovative and surprising solutions to their problems—solutions that did not just require increased dollar spending to be effective. We still relied on the experience we had gotten working on large accounts at large agencies. But we combined this with our newfound small agency ability to get meaningful marketing results for our clients based not on the media that was purchased, but rather on the power of the ideas—strategic but unexpected—that were created. So we knew who we thought we were. It felt right because it truly came out of who we had become. It was different from the way most other agencies positioned themselves. It did seem as if, with the right combination of words, our business could be made to be seem truly distinctive. In short, we needed a good idea. (Does that need sound familiar?)

Here are some samples of actual slogans I created in those early days and wrote down as contenders, some more seriously than others:

1. Making large agencies nervous since 1993.
2. Our business is growing your business.
3. Do you know how much a large agency would charge for the stuff we do?
4. Small agency thinking.
5. Scaring large agencies since 1993.
6. The small agency that makes you look big.
7. Big agency intelligence. Small agency smarts.
8. Big agency thinking. Small agency guile.
9. Twice as large as a one-man shop.

If we had done what I encourage you to do—develop a strategy first, develop ideas later—then the elimination process would have been a lot simpler. But like you, we were in a hurry to get back to running our business. Unlike you, I had spent a career doing this, so I could sense what was good and what wasn't, at least to me. I knew the strategy, though never written or formalized, was to convince potential clients that our experience at large agencies made us good at all the stuff that big agencies do (strategic positioning, powerful creative). But now that we had spent some time working with clients with smaller budgets, we had learned how to communicate the marketing message in ways that did not depend on bloated budgets. So, based on that, which of the above do you think did the best job?

The answer, sort of, was "Big agency thinking. Small agency guile." I say, "sort of," because as we thought about it "guile" didn't seem like the ideal word. It had connotations of cleverness in tricking or deceiving people, and that was not the talent we were particularly good at or wanted to offer.

So our final "Here's who we are and here's what we offer that makes us different" winner was "Big agency thinking. Small agency ingenuity." It was a combination of words that we liked and felt was a good idea.

4

WHERE ARE YOU GOING?

What do you want with a good idea anyway? You may have been doing fine up to now, so why bother?

Perhaps it is because there is someone out there who is getting the business you know you should be getting. Perhaps he provides better service or gives higher discounts. Or his customers just think he's better. The reason they think that might be because he is letting customers and prospects know about him by using, pardon the expression, good ideas to make his company stand out.

Well, that's one reason you might want to get some good ideas: to give yourself an advantage over the competition. But there are other reasons too. You have to identify them and select the most important reason to answer the question of what you intend to do with your idea, because knowing what you intend to do with your idea will help you determine what your idea should be. What do you hope to accomplish? What do you want the idea to do? If you don't know where you want to go, how will you know if you get there?

Do you want to:

1. Build a specific piece of your business?
2. Expand your market?
3. Increase your market share?
4. Enthuse your salespeople?
5. Sell more Phufkels?
6. Sell an improved Phufkel?
7. Let more people know you exist?
8. Change a customer's perception of your company?
9. Make your business appear bigger?
10. Get your foot (or other body part) in the door?

There are as many reasons as there are businesses. But in no case is the answer: all of the above. The more single-minded and focused the strategy (and that is what you are developing: a strategy), the more likely the ideas you generate based on that strategy will be compelling, persuasive, and unique. If your strategy (what you have decided you want to accomplish) is simply "I want to sell more Phufkels," then almost any idea you come up with will fit that vague thought. The idea will probably be as bland as the strategy. But if your strategy is more in the manner of "I want to let customers know my Phufkel now comes in purple," then your ideas will be more tailored, focused, and effective. Of course, be careful of becoming mired in too much detail, such as: "I want to let customers know my Phufkel now comes in purple, folds in half, and has a new plastic covering."

Good Idea: This is a very long chapter. It is an important chapter, but the kind I never could really read myself without the "eye glaze" that also comes from reading long, descriptive passages weighted down with adjectives. Here is what you can do if you suffer from the same problem that I have. For the moment, just read this small Good Idea section and then continue on with the rest of the book. Later, if you want, you can come back and read the entire chapter. If not, I won't be upset. It is *The Princess Bride* approach to avoiding reader boredom. Simply stated, decide:

- Who you are trying to talk to (your audience)?
- What are you trying to tell them about your Phufkel (your message)?
- What do you want them to do (their actions)?

- **What reason(s) have you given them to do it (your benefits)?**

  Okay? Now, for those of you so inclined, here is the rest of this chapter.

Often you will find that the best way to devise a strategy is simply to determine the parameters of the problem that you want your idea to solve. Thinking about what you want your idea to accomplish in terms of a problem to solve is a good approach. Then you can develop your strategy as a solution to your problem.

If you look at the earlier list and couch the questions as problems to solve, it may make the process clearer.

1. My problem is not how to increase sales all across the board, but how to increase sales in one segment.
2. My problem is how to expand my target audience.
3. My problem is that I don't have a large enough presence in the marketplace.
4. My problem is the complacency of my sales team.
5. My problem in that I have excess inventory.
6. My problem is lack of product innovation.
7. My problem is that not enough people know about my company.
8. My problem is that my customers have the wrong perception of my company.
9. My problem is people think I am too small to meet all their needs.
10. My problem is not knowing how to make the initial contact.

The strategy is what you judge your good idea against to make certain that the good idea is not just clever for the sake of clever, but actually comes out of the strategy and solves the problem

Developing a strategy will help you know what you intend to communicate—it's not the idea, words, or art at this point, but just a guide. Strategies are not strait jackets. They do not rigidly confine you to one path and restrict your creative output. It is actually the opposite. Strategies open up your creative possibilities, help guide you though the many routes you could take, and focus on the correct one. I must confess I like a good strategy. It helps me to understand how to judge my ideas. While it will not measure the quality of the idea, it will help determine, out of infinite creative possibilities, which will best fit the strategy. In the examples above, the strategies might be:

1. To increase sales in one segment.
2. To find a new target audience.
3. To expand my presence in the marketplace.
4. To inspire and motivate my sales team.
5. To eliminate excess inventory.
6. To communicate product innovations.
7. To increase and improve my marketing communications so that more prospects will learn about my company.
8. To communicate the proper company image to my customers.
9. To communicate the benefits of how my size allows me to better service my customers.
10. To devise communications that will help me reach new prospects.

Once you develop a strategy you are happy with, you will then have to answer other essential questions: Whom are you talking to, and what do you intend to tell them? In other words, after you determine who *you* are and the strategy you will be using to reach your audience, you have to figure out who *they* are. Who is your target; who is it that you want to purchase your Phufkel?

You can define your target audience in any way or ways that are meaningful to you. But you face the same concerns that you did when defining your strategy. If your target audience, as defined by you, is as vague as "people who might buy my Phufkels, I hope, I hope" you have to give this topic additional thought. If you describe your strategy as "I want to sell more Phufkels to married women with children," then your ideas will be focused and more likely to be effective because you can visualize your target more clearly. Of course, you must also be careful of defining the target too specifically: "I want to sell more Phufkels to women on Tuesday afternoons, every other month, while it is raining."

Looking at your possible audience in various ways will help you define your target. Some ways to categorize them even have very impressive names, like "demographics" or "psychographics." This targeting topic is so important that there are entire books devoted to this one issue.

Some of the numerous ways you might consider thinking about your target, depending upon what your Phufkel actually is, might be:

- ◆ Age (How old are they, what do their toys look like, are their bones strong, are they retired)
- ◆ Income (rich, poor, really rich, on a fixed budget; would your Phufkel be a necessity or a luxury)
- ◆ Lifestyle (carefree, conservative, campers, rock-climbers, readers)

◆ Attitude (squirrel it away, spend money like water)
◆ Geography (local, overseas, coastal, warm, rainy)
◆ Business (private, public, size, corporate culture)

Remember, it is not the quantity of people you talk to, it is the quality. What might help is if you actually try to picture this person, because he is the one for whom you are doing all the work. Don't picture a group; just picture one person. (I realize it is difficult to picture one person who is 18–34, but you know what I mean.) This practice will help you focus your message so you do not waste words, money, and the effort of getting your marketing message to those other people who will never care. As Carol Super says in her book, *Selling (Without Selling)*,"I literally leave the room at some point during our discussion. From outside the doorway, I explain that many more people can now hear what I'm saying, but only the people in the room are at all interested. . . . " It is the same with you and your target audience. If your Phufkel only works on long hair, it makes little sense to focus on military personnel as your target. So define your target carefully. Make a list of who might want to listen to the marketing message you will be creating. Is it a current client, a previous one, or a new prospect? Why would the target want your Phufkel?

 Good Idea: Make a drawing of an actual round target with five or six concentric circles, the kind stuffed with straw that Robin Hood shot arrows into. On the outermost circle, start to define your target audience. Imprecise is okay at this point, just write down general characteristics you think that your target has. Then go to the next smaller circle and refine your definition. Make it a little more descriptive and more precise. Keep moving in, thinking, and writing, and by the time you get to the bull's-eye you should have a pretty accurate feeling for the person/group/association that would make the most sense to spend money and effort to go after. (The "most sense" meaning the most likely to have a need for and be able to afford and actually want your Phufkel.) Or, if I dare say it, the group that would provide the best ROI (return on investment) for you.

Sometimes the target is obvious and can be easily seen. Often, sadly, it is not quite that clear. Let's say your Phufkel is a new chocolate candy bar with gummy worms embedded in it. Who do you think your target might be? The kids who would actually eat the candy? The moms who might buy it for them? Both the kids and the parents? Maybe it's for boys only? Or just girls? Teens? Children? If you could afford it, research would be helpful to learn about purchasing patterns in the category, competitive products, and other important pieces of information. This is an important area, and you should spend time and effort coming up with the right decision. It will make the work you do later much easier. Selecting the proper target impacts many of your other choices: what the message should be, what media to purchase, and pricing. It works together with the strategy. It is your well thought out plan of how you will achieve your goal and reach your target. The correct strategy for the previous candy bar/gummy example would tell you which of the possible targets makes the most sense. Once you decide on the proper target, the strategy will help you decide on the proper creative for that audience. Is the target more important than your strategy? More important than a good idea? Don't ask me, you already know my answer.

Here's a real world strategic issue for you: There need not be one penny spent on focus groups or research. Just use your gut feeling. Here's the background.

In Manhattan, there is a branch library on Fifth Avenue, between 40th and 41st streets. For as long as I can remember, there has been someone selling used books on the 40th Street corner, next to the library. His target is obvious; people who go to the library like to read and enjoy books, so it makes sense those are the people a street vendor would go after. But the strategic question is this: Is he better off trying to sell his books to people who can get all the free books they want just by going inside the library and checking them out? Or would a better strategy be to move his cart to a different corner, where he might get increased pedestrian traffic and would have no competition from the library? It is an interesting question for you to think about, and it has a real world answer.

The answer is that it is obviously better to offer his books close to the library. How can I know this? Because he is still there. If it were not a good strategy and he was not selling plenty of books, he would have moved years ago to a better location.

CASE HISTORY: RALSTON PURINA'S HERO DOG FOOD

When I was working on creating an ad campaign for dog food products for Ralston Purina, one assignment was for a new dog food, code name Brutus, final name Hero. The way it was different from other dog foods was that it was specifically formulated for the nutritional needs of large-breed dogs. We knew where we would be going, strategically. Certainly we could be confident of the target we would be going after; it would make little sense to go after owners of small-breed or medium-breed dogs. Simple, huh? But it is never as simple as that. There were still important strategic and targeting questions that had to be answered.

Good Idea: Write down all the questions you can think of that you feel you would want the answers to before you started working on Hero Dog Food. As someone once said, there are no dumb questions. (Notice they left out silly, inane, and stupid.) Keep in mind what you do know: You are going after owners of large-breed dogs with a product made specifically for their pets. Any other information you would like?

Though your list of questions is undoubtedly different, here are the kinds of questions that I wanted to have answered, without knowing if any of the answers were important or would lead to anything creative:

- ♦ Is there a geographic difference among owners of large-breed dogs?
- ♦ Do large-breed dog owners tend to be younger? Older?
- ♦ Is there a difference in gender of large-breed dog owners?
- ♦ Do large-breed dog owners tend to have more than one dog? All the same size?
- ♦ Are large-breed dog owners "big" themselves?
- ♦ How important is it to provide complete nutritional formulation in the advertising?

♦ Is it important to reference the ailments that large-breed dogs are prone to (for example, hip dysplasia)?
♦ How exactly are the nutritional needs of large-breed dogs different?

To get the answers to these and other questions we did research, quantitative and qualitative. We conducted focus groups, which is where you bring in a group of consumers and observe their reactions to product questions and samples, usually through a two-way mirror. After the focus groups and after reading the other research, I came away with some strong feelings.

One, the group believed Ralston Purina was a reputable company. They thought it stood for healthy, nutritionally sound pet products. Also, while they were not quite certain why large-breed dogs had different nutritional needs than smaller dogs—Did Goliath eat differently than David, other than the amount?—they were willing to believe it, given their trust in Ralston Purina. Finally, the groups confirmed that pet owners have strong emotional attachments to their animals.

The heritage of Ralston Purina and the relationship owners had with their large pets made it clear to me that while it should be emotional, it also should be fun. After all, big dogs can get into larger dilemmas and seem to have a different relationship with their owners than tiny dogs do. My slogan (and jingle) was simple enough: "Hero Dog Food. If You've Got A Big Dog." When it came to the announcer copy, we just provided the reassurance that Hero Dog Food was specifically made for the nutritional needs of large-breed dogs. This abbreviated announcer copy allowed me more time in each spot to humanize each scene. Each commercial in the campaign, selected to introduce the brand in the test markets, had a series of vignettes. In each scene a person, addressing the camera, started his story with: My dog is so big. . . ." Each statement was completed in a different, fun visual way. For example, in one commercial there was a guy in a car, with his large-breed dog's head sticking through the opening in the roof. His line was, "My dog is so big, I had to buy a car with a sunroof." Another scene had a girl in exercise clothing doing sit-ups with her large dog lying horizontally across her knees, helping to hold her legs down. As she came to the top of her sit-up she told the viewer, "My dog is so big, he helps me with my exercise." There was the young girl in a bathing suit standing behind her soaking wet Irish setter on the beach. As she said, "My dog is so big. . . ." on cue the dog shook off the water, soaking the poor girl, who never finished her line but just broke up laughing.

So I knew whom the audience was (owners of large-breed dogs) and what I was trying to tell them about the Phufkel (this product was specially formulated for those dogs), and I gave them a reason to believe it (Ralston Purina made it). All of it tied up inside a good idea.

5

WORK VERY HARD.
ONCE.

Here's my confession: I am, without doubt, as lazy as the laziest of you. I will procrastinate, go for a stroll, count my corkscrews . . . anything at all rather than face the demanding task of coming up with a good idea. I am not ashamed to admit it. I have learned that the result of knowing I am lazy is that I force myself to work as hard as possible in the beginning, not stopping till I have come up with a good idea. I know how much easier that will make everything else later on.

If you are lazy, lack confidence in your ability to produce good ideas, or are just too busy or preoccupied to spend a lot of time trying to come up with an idea—even though you recognize its importance—here's what I am asking you to do. Work very hard just one time to develop your ideas. Because—and here's the best part, the motivation, the promise—once you have a good idea, the rest is reasonably easy. Honest.

Working hard "once" does not necessarily mean at one sitting or one attempt. It does mean working *really* hard. Really, really hard. It means looking, reading, writing, researching, and more, all the while dealing with that frustrating problem known as creating.

However, the knowledge that the rest will be that proverbial piece of cake is a tasty carrot to keep you going, to jumble together a few food clichés. There are a lot of chapters ahead on what to do with your good idea. You will find ways to improve your idea, get more mileage out of it, make it sing. But it is all predicated on having a good idea in the first place.

Everyone has different work habits. You may prefer to do the easy tasks first before tackling the hard work. You may fret about the mechanics of a project, rather than worry about the content. No matter what your usual work technique, there really is no way to avoid the effort involved in coming up with a good idea.

The idea will become the foundation of everything to follow, which is why we are spending so much time figuring out where to get one. Again, I promise, the harder you work on this, the easier everything else will be.

CASE HISTORY: OXYDOL DETERGENT

Oxydol was a washing machine detergent. When I worked on the Oxydol ad campaign it was marketed by Procter & Gamble. As P&G products almost always do, it had a product difference. Oxydol's difference was that it was not just a plain detergent; it also contained bleaching crystals. And to make sure customers were aware of that difference, they colored some of the crystals green, so people could see the bleach.

Good Idea: Does your Phufkel have a color that could highlight its difference? Could you add a color to give it the appearance of being different? One client had a proprietary video camera, with many built in bells and the accompanying whistles. But looking at it, you couldn't see it was different, let alone better. So the suggestion was made to paint the camera a color—almost any color except the standard black—that would visually support the premise that this was different from ordinary video cameras.

The strategy was simply to convince women that Oxydol detergent got clothes whiter than other detergents because it contained bleaching crystals. You could, and I am sure the ad agency I was with at the time did, spend forever on executions that talked about green bleaching crystals that promised to give your clothes a superior whiteness or the idea that no extra bleach has to be added because Oxydol already has bleaching crystals in the box. I am sure we looked at all the expected areas for the category: like "Mom, if you really care about getting your family's clothes clean," or "Watch this stain disappear," or other classic benefits.

We created and explored those executions because that was where the strategy that had been agreed upon logically led you. And if your Phufkels have the same budgets that Procter & Gamble products usually have, well, it may not matter quite as much what you say, because you will be able to say it often enough that people will at least hear the message. Of course the better the idea, the more effective the media. But if you have a limited budget, you have to do something different—still on strategy, but out of the ordinary.

At the time I was as green as Oxydol's bleaching crystals; I was a new copywriter recently added to an established team. My chief priority was impressing my boss, not actually caring if I sold a commercial to the client (short-sighted *and* stupid, like two mints in one). So I worked really hard, exploring all the ideas I thought my boss would like. That is, all the trite, cliché ideas I thought would show I knew the formula for writing commercials, because the ideas were indirectly lifted from every bad detergent commercial I had ever seen. I wrote and I wrote. I worked at night and got into the cubicle early every morning. And the result?

Not even one possibly good idea. Nothing that seemed fresh, new, compelling. Since I wasn't really trying to do well, was merely trying to anticipate what others might like, it was most unlikely that I would ever have found a good idea, or recognized it if it had miraculously appeared. I suppose my boss knew I was trying for safe rather than good, because one Friday he told me to go home and come back Monday with something really good. I was challenged to stick with the strategy but throw out all other rules, actual or self-imposed. I went home determined to come up with an idea that I actually believed in, because even if no one else liked it at least I could finally feel comfortable defending its merit. And that was perhaps the first time I realized that all the hard work is worth it at the end, even—or especially—when you discard all the bad ideas that you have created in the beginning. I found that you have to go through the process, developing and discarding the terrible stuff, to allow you to finally create and appreciate the good ideas that will finally appear. Part of the process is learning how to tell the difference between a good and bad idea. Or an idea that at first glance seems fresh and powerful, till you try to mold it into shape. Or an idea you are not sure about, but discover that with a little twist, a bit of polish it actually is pretty good.

Good Idea: Once you have done all the preliminary thinking and have truly tried very hard to come up with a good idea, a good, clean honest idea, then walk away. Take a break. Relax. Play with your kids. Enjoy a nap. One of the nice things about ideas is that you don't even have to be in front of your computer when they show up. The point is to let your creative subconscious do some work. You will be amazed what it will often come up with, without even expecting a raise or recognition for its efforts.

That weekend I did come up with lots of ideas, some actually good. The one I especially liked broke just about every Procter & Gamble rule. But it was indeed based on the strategy that had been agreed to: that Oxydol got clothes whiter than other detergents thanks to its bleaching crystals. And I had not seen anything like it. Well, I might have, since it was a satire of a clothes-cleaning contest. But I didn't really remember ever seeing any specific cleaning contest on television. It was like the cartoons you see of a school kid sitting in a corner of a classroom, wearing a cone-shaped dunce cap. While a rare few have actually ever seen this, it is immediately accepted as true to life.

What I came up with was a fictional Mrs. Housewife contest. There was a group of women, each standing in front of her washing machine. On the top of each machine was a box of detergent, whose identity was concealed by a brown paper wrapper. The announcer began by telling the audience the results of the contest. He announced the winner, and that's when the fun started. The other contestants started loudly complaining as they converged on the winner, ripping the wrapper from her box to reveal it was a box of Oxydol. They said things like, "Hey, it isn't fair," "Look, green bleaching crystals. It must be Oxydol," "Of course she won" (meaning of course she got her clothes whiter/cleaner), "Take the bleach out. Then her detergent would be more like mine," (meaning it would be less effective)," and "We were told to play fair." And as they continued to close in, mildly menacing the winner, the voice over announcer told the world, "Oxydol, with its green bleaching crystals, gets clothes so white. . . [The next three words went up on the screen as a title next to the box of Oxydol as the announcer finished] It Isn't Fair."

For a Procter & Gamble commercial it was certainly unexpected. As was the slogan, "It Isn't Fair." After all, it wasn't a benefit line or even truly a claim. It wasn't even a complete thought by itself. But it certainly implied a lot, relying on the common sense of the viewers to easily fill in for themselves the benefits and superiority of Oxydol. It certainly made its point about the superiority of Oxydol, thanks to its single-minded focus on the difference the green bleaching crystals made in the end result. Even today I can't quite believe that this idea ever was produced. But Procter & Gamble recognized a good—though unusual—idea and used the power of testing and research to confirm their opinion.

You can see the power of working really hard, just once. That full weekend of extra effort produced an idea that took off on a journey of its own. The basic idea, "Oxydol Gets Clothes So White, It Isn't Fair," ended up running on television for years, eventually using Pat Carroll, an actress and exceptional comedienne, as the spokesperson. The reason the idea could alter its visuals, format, and execution was simple. It was a good idea in the first place, even if it wasn't found in the first place I looked (or the twentieth). I guess it is like someone searching for gold. He will put up with a lot of hard work knowing that there is a good chance the reward, if unearthed, will be worth it. As will the search for a good idea.

6

WHERE DO YOU FIND A GOOD IDEA?

Look, there's a good idea, next to the lamp. And over there, behind the desk, there's another one. I don't mean that literally. But you will discover that ideas are out there, waiting to be discovered by you, burnished by you, sharpened and shaped by you.

The development of creating good ideas can be broken down into simple, manageable steps. Don't worry if your ideas at first seem, well, familiar, obvious, even, dare we say it, dull! Once you start to jot them down you'll see how other ideas start to flow.

If you apply the guidance from the following chapters, you will see how to improve a run-of-the-mill idea, perk it up, and turn it into something to be proud of.

Keep in mind at some point the creation of the idea will be the most important part of the process, but not yet. The first few attempts will help to get you familiar and comfortable with the process: finding the ideas, writing them down, making them as clear as possible, then as creative as possible. Later we'll worry about using the whole carcass and turning an idea from nice to good, but not yet. As Anne Lamott says in her book on writing (and life), *Bird by Bird*, "Don't worry about doing it well yet, though. Just start getting it down."

It is natural to feel unprepared and insecure and think that your ideas will never be quite good enough. If all this is new to you, you will undoubtedly be even more anxious. That is what always happens during the creative process, and it's usually followed by "I will never have a good idea again." Well, let's hope you do, especially if it is your first.

I remember talking to Adolph Green, who, along with his partner Betty Comden, wrote the lyrics to *On The Town*, *Wonderful Town*, and *Bells Are Ringing*, to name just a few of their many famous musical collaborations. I asked Adolph about the screenplay they had written for *Singin' in the Rain*, which is on most lists of the ten best movies. I was curious if it had just flowed out effortlessly, because the finished product was so seamless. Adolph, who had many successes under his belt, said that what happened during the writing of this screenplay was exactly what happened every time he and Betty got involved with a project. At some point early in the process they would go to the producer and tell him that they just couldn't do it, none of their ideas were good enough, and could they please return their salary and just go back to New York!

The point is if legendary figures with track records like Comden and Green had their creative anxiety, you are certainly entitled to yours. Hopefully, like them, your ideas will flourish.

Sometimes, of course, the idea will just pop up and seem so natural, logical, and clever you immediately recognize it is a good idea.

LOOK INSIDE

Gather any marketing pieces that your company has done, past and current: ads—trade and consumer, print and television—brochures, websites, sell sheets, media kits, direct mailings. Yes, everything.

Read them and write down any thoughts, lines, or ideas that you think have merit. Again, this is *not* to pilfer or poach, but to be stimulated by or perhaps be disappointed with, but most assuredly to be aware of what to stay away from. You might see something that prompts a notion that jumps out at you that wasn't thought of before. Write it down!

Good Idea: Take the brochure, ad, mailing piece, or whatever you are looking over and rewrite it. I don't mean change it; I literally mean copy it. What happens is that this forces you to really look at and think about the words and why they flow the way they do. When you just look it over, no matter how carefully you think you are examining it, you will often slide over words and phrases not realizing that what you think you read is not what was on the page. Copying it gives you a good feel for the rhythm and voice of the piece, which could lead you somewhere interesting. Also, depending upon how industrious you are, how serious you are, and how much time you have, consider looking at your stationery, your business cards, even your company's slogan if one exists. If you are looking to create a good idea, perhaps starting at the most obvious level is not such a bad idea.

Now that you have examined, written down, and thoroughly pored over what your company is doing, how about speaking to your employees? Or if you are an employee, why not talk to your coworkers. Ask them what they think about your company's Phufkels, what makes them seem better, different and how the marketing could be improved. Ask them what they really like about their Phufkels and do they feel the truly important points are being communicated? Is there a feature that they feel your competition doesn't have and that should be more prominent in the marketing?

This does not necessarily need to be more than casual water-cooler conversation. It is not a formal "Let's have a meeting and decide on a new five-year marketing plan." What you are looking for are insights and viewpoints that are different from yours, from individuals who probably have different agendas, styles, and ideas that are different than yours.

How about looking for informed ideas inside your company by speaking to your suppliers? This could be everyone from the person who does your printing to whomever makes parts for your Phufkel, your outside insurance/health plan providers—everyone. They will have viewpoints that are broader, and ideas that are different than yours. Certainly they will be more objective (even if you are a major source of their income). They can quickly deflate any grandiose ideas you have as to why the whole world should insist on using only your Phufkels.

At this point you have looked at your marketing materials and spoken to your employees and suppliers. Now how about your customers? They are the ones you have already convinced of the benefits and superiority of your Phufkel. Wouldn't you like to know why they are your customers? It may not always be because of your wonderful service or low prices or your winning personality. The reason for their patronage could be, sadly, as simple as inertia. Finding out from them what they think, not only of your marketing, but of your Phfukel itself can be interesting, especially if there is a disconnect between what your marketing communicates to them and what they actually think your Phufkel does.

LOOK OUTSIDE

Now that you have looked inside, reviewing your own current marketing materials, researching your industry's advertising, and speaking to your clients, employees, and suppliers, is there anything else to do before developing your good ideas? If you looked closely at this section heading, then you already know the answer. It is time for you to look outside your business. You will find it is a similar process, but instead of being on the inside looking in, you are on the inside looking out.

Look at your competitor's websites, advertising, and marketing materials. They shouldn't be hard to find. Someone in your company may know people who work with your competitors or might have even worked there at one point. Certainly you can pick up materials at your Phufkel trade show. (Don't be surprised if your competition is examining what you have to say in your own show materials.)

Good Idea: Next time you go to a trade show or conference—in fact, every time you go—spend time looking at what your competition is doing. Preferably without judging their efforts (*Those dopes, don't they know that trend is over, that next year's Phufkels will all be three inches shorter*). See what their signage is saying and what is different or new in what they are offering and featuring. Pick up copies of all their marketing materials. Get on their mailing list. Introduce yourself to those you don't know and chat them up. We know you will be smart enough not to reveal anything that shouldn't be talked about. But we don't know about them, do we?

Go back to your suppliers who you have asked for insights into your marketing and ask them about your competition as well. What type of marketing materials are they receiving from them? What do they think about their Phufkels, and do they know of any improvements for the coming season? Again, this is to get information to help you improve your business, not to poach someone else's hard work.

Here is an example of where looking outside your own category can lead. My advertising agency recently had a meeting with an architectural firm. The meeting was intended to be a preliminary "getting to know you" meeting. But I walked away with the point of view that where this company was different was that they not only knew how to design uncommonly attractive commercial buildings, but they also knew how to use that design to maximize the leasing space available and hence the profits for the owners. While I did not have intimate knowledge of the industry, the terminology, or the competitive landscape, this seemed like a possible direction to explore for a good idea. (Remember, we had had only one meeting and did not know if other ad agencies were being interviewed or even how serious they were about hiring one. But it is somehow comforting to me to have developed at least one idea—or failing that, a notion—that could be the basis for a good idea if someone shook me awake at night saying they needed an idea by the next day and that we would only get their business if we had a campaign by 8 A.M. As it is said, only the paranoid survive.)

Later that week I was reading an article about airlines and the industry's need to balance profits and innovation. I realized that this was in many ways analogous to the architectural firm's dilemma. At one extreme, an airline could decide to squeeze as many seats as possible into every airplane, charging the highest fares possible, to maximize revenue. Or they could decide to eliminate a meaningful number of seats, designing the interior to maximize the comfort of the passengers on each flight. That is in essence the decision an architectural firm had to make every time it designed a building: design freedom versus revenue. Looking at these factors from the outside, thinking about them from a different perspective—that of an airline—could lead to unexpected ideas and creative solutions for the architectural firm.

CASE HISTORY: PREVENT BLINDNESS NY

Peter Freidfeld of ClearVison Optical asked if I would take on a *pro bono* assignment for Prevent Blindness NY, an organization dedicated to finding ways of preventing blindness and preserving sight. What they wanted was a tag line or slogan for their marketing materials. Peter told me afterward that what I created for them was not at all what they expected. They had been expecting something along the lines of "Prevent Blindness NY. It is up to you." Or for something more creative, maybe "Prevent Blindness NY. See your way clear."

I had spoken with key people at the organization for their input, looked at their website, and read their materials. Then as I went through my informal research I looked outside, where I discovered one fundamental problem. As I spoke to my coworkers, family members, and friends for guidance as to what they thought of Prevent Blindness compared to other organizations for the visually impaired, one thing became obvious: Almost everyone I spoke to thought it was impossible to prevent blindness.

They believed they understood what The Lighthouse did, for example. It provided training, along with products specifically designed for the visually impaired, such as special playing cards, clocks, magnifying mirrors, talking products, and special computers.

Another organization that deals with the vision impaired, the Helen Keller Foundation, was believed by most to serve the needs of the blind and those with vision loss using research, education, and training. But an organization that could show how to actually prevent blindness, my outside panel thought? No way. This doubt is what led me to the phrase that was eventually used. The good idea was to take the fact that most people don't think they can actually prevent blindness by telling them they actually could. When we said "prevent blindness," and they subconsciously said, "No, you can't," my line answered their unspoken doubts with "Yes, you really can." Which is why the new slogan was "Prevent Blindness NY. (Yes, You Really Can.)" There actually were, and are, things that can be done: Research, vision awareness programs, school wide vision testing at a young age to detect, delay, and prevent future problems. But if I hadn't spoken to real people and "looked outside" I never would have realized the depths of skepticism that existed and would never have found that good idea.

Good Idea: Instead of just looking at your own industry's advertising and your competition, look outside your category. Are you selling a high-end luxury product? Well, what are the expensive liquor companies or high-end automotive companies doing in their marketing that might have some application to yours? If you are in the fast-food business, don't stop your "looking outside" by just examining what McDonald's or Burger King are doing. How about seeing what other companies that have similar price points in their category, like inexpensive footwear, economical hotels, or low-cost airlines are doing? Have any of them discovered a selling point that might also make sense to your customers and would be very distinctive in your category? As Mayor Bloomberg said, regarding the Paris bike rental program, in the *New York Times* "You try to see whether it fits, and some parts of it will, but it may very well give you an idea to do something totally different." Again, thou shalt not steal!

CASE HISTORY: KANGOL CAPS

One of my assignments was creating an ad for Kangol caps, which would have been more enjoyable if they hadn't wanted the ad to be for their golf caps, to appear in golfing magazines, and appeal to golfers. If you are an avid golfer this task might have been easy for you, but not for me. I have played golf twice in my life, both times at a pitch-and-putt par 3 course. Unless you count rounds of miniature golf with my kids, those two outings are about the sum total of my experience and knowledge of the game. It's not that I necessarily agree with Mark Twain's sentiment that "Golf is a good walk, spoiled." It's just that I come from Brooklyn, which to me is reason enough for my lack of interest. (Stickball is a different story, however.) Since I knew nothing about the sport, I looked inside—read golf magazines and looked at golf columns. I spoke to everyone I knew who knew something about golf. After listening to golf enthusiasts, looking at golf ads, and doing all the things I suggest you do, I had a fair amount of information along with some insights, but I still did not have a decent idea. The important learning came when I went "outside," asking people questions

about sports in general. I discussed baseball, football, soc-
cer, basketball, and even stoopball and finally something
clicked. I realized the one element people believed all
these various sports had in common was that the better
players all had enormous awareness and focus. Superior
players—no matter the particular game—analyzed,
examined, and scrutinized themselves, their team's performance, and the competition, looking for the small
edge that could make all the difference. I realized how
this applied to golf, which led me, finally, to the good
idea. It was an ad split on two facing pages, which wasn't
such a bad idea in itself. On the outside top quarter of the
left page was the question, "What's the most important
thing in golf . . .?" Opposite that question, on the outside
top corner of the right page, was the answer: "How you
use your head." This was accompanied by a close shot of
a man wearing a Kangol golf cap. That, along with some
short body copy, was the ad. A good idea, but it was in a
category that I had no real feel for, until I went outside.

7

BEING CLEAR IS
A GOOD IDEA

The purpose of a good idea is *not* to show the world how clever you are. I'm sure you have seen some ideas that are too clever by far, making you feel you need a roadmap or thesaurus to figure out what they are trying to say. *A good idea is never convoluted, obscure, or impenetrable.* By definition — or at least my definition — it can't be a good idea if it is confusing. A good idea can be cryptic, and it can be intriguing; it can't be irrelevant or puzzling. If you are so enamored with your ingenuity you truly believe the reader will be willing to wade through your verbiage just to get to your oh-so-clever payoff, you will be oh-so-wrong. The point of a good idea, never to be forgotten, is to sell more Phufkels. Being clever will help your good idea stand out and be noticed. Being too clever may reward your ego, but it will do little for your sales. Clear does not mean dull, safe, or obvious. But it does mean your idea communicates what you want it to; it conveys the message you have determined has the best chance of getting attention. In short, being clear is often surprisingly more effective than you might suppose. While clarity can lead to a good idea, it often can be a good idea in itself. That's why it is not a waste of your time to write down ideas that seem simple and obvious to you. They won't necessarily be simple and obvious to your target. At the very least your message should be straightforward and convey what you intend to communicate. That is a pretty important step. To get to the simple, clear statement, whether to be used as a starting point or the actual headline, it might help you to ask some questions, such as those that reporters often use to determine fundamental facts.

♦ **Who**. As in to whom is your message directed? The wholesaler, the trade, the ultimate consumers? In other words, who is your target?

♦ **What**. What are you trying to say about your Phufkel? What is the news or information you want to convey? What are the benefits? Will your Phufkel make life easier, save people money, increase longevity? Can you think of one, two, six facts about your Phufkels that your competitors couldn't say about their Phufkels? Or, if the benefits aren't truly unique to your Phufkel, can you at least state them with more authority and believability based on your businesses history and brand's personality?

♦ **When**. The truth is deadlines often dictate results. Do you need this piece of communication right away or do you have some time to polish your message and get it in better shape? Is it for a trade show that has a definite date or can you wait a while? Is it past the magazine's "drop dead date," (the last possible moment you can get material to the publication) or can you spend a little more time improving it?

♦ **Why**. Always a good question. Why are you looking for a good idea? Do you have real news or specific news? Are you responding to what a competitor is doing? Announcing a new/lower priced/improved Phufkel? Or are you simply bored with your current marketing materials?

♦ **Where**. Where is the idea going to be used? Is it for a letterhead? Or a blog? A sign for your window? A television spot? A full color, back cover of a national magazine? It does matter. But in my opinion, it does not matter as much as you might think.

For example, here is an idea that was perhaps a wee bit too clever. I was having a yard sale and, as you can imagine by now, was not content to simply run an ad that headlined, "Yard Sale." My ad in the local paper proclaimed, "I Am Selling All The Stuff I Bought At Your Yard Sale." The resulting crowd was okay; stuff was sold, books given away. Were the results any better or different than if I had taken the more traditional route and wording? I don't know. Part of me says it was clever where being witty was neither called for, expected, or beneficial. On the other creative hand, there is something to be said for trying to be creative at every opportunity; the exercise is beneficial, and the more you do it the easier it becomes.

 Good Idea: When you have some ideas and have turned them into what appear to be good ideas, try these two exercises. First, try to make them even cleverer. Second, try the reverse. Try to make them as clear as can be, aiming for an understandable, uncomplicated communication, not a shot at an award. If this makes them dull and expected and not even slightly surprising, then go with the clever. But uncomplicated and straightforward may lead to a more compelling and powerful message.

We did a marketing project once for Gideon and Schein, a company that does, well, that's part of the example. When they came to us they were using a brochure that featured a definition of what their business was. They were "Family Office Consultants." Got it? Know anyone who would want to hire them for their services? Okay, how about if I tell you their one-sentence definition of the services they offered: "Making life easier through expert, one-on-one management of your personal, office and financial affairs."

Want to hire them? Probably not, especially if you found out, as I did, that the most important service they provided was managing all kinds of personal and legal matters for seniors and that they did it at the clients' homes.

Following is the definition of their business that I created for them: "In-Home Administrators For Seniors." My explanation of their services became: "Providing Management And Coordination Of Personal, Financial, Legal And Health Insurance Matters." (You still may not want their services, but at least I am confident you know what they are offering to do for you.)

Because I was concerned that some people would still think they were simply accountants, I came up with a slogan to further define and differentiate them: "Life Keeping, Not Just Bookkeeping." (Actually, I came up with "Not Just Bookkeeping. Life Keeping." The client, correctly, changed it to "Life Keeping, Not Just Bookkeeping," to start the thought off with a positive and to put the important news first.)

To give an example of how the little details mean a lot, they told us that shortly after that they were attending a trade show where they purchased booth space—a small booth that was basically a table, a few chairs, and a wall behind them to promote their services. They knew they would be surrounded, as they had been in the past, by larger companies, well-known eldercare attorneys, insurance and annuity companies, and the like, all with much larger budgets and more elaborate booths. As my client pointed out, they did not have the budget to stand out from these larger organizations.

As we now know, the budget is not the important factor in your marketing, what matters is the idea. Here was mine.

I suggested to Gideon and his partner Rebecca that they not try to make a fancy booth. Rather, they should focus their efforts on doing something that reflected one of the more important components of who they were and what they offered. That is, that they were *in-home* administrators. Why not design their booth to look as if they were in a room in someone's home? It could be a modern, contemporary but still "homey" room. All it took was the proper table cloth, a picture frame, some flowers, and a few other inexpensive accessories that drove home the "in-home" difference, saved money, and still looked as if they designed the booth to look like a home on purpose, not because of a lack of funds but because they chose to make that statement.

They took my advice, and the most interesting feedback they received was from the woman who organized the trade show. She told them that this was the first time she understood what their company actually did.

CASE HISTORY: DALLAS BBQ

Dallas BBQ is a collection of eight BBQ restaurants located in New York. It is a third generation, family-owned business. When they hired my agency a decade ago, they were about to open a Dallas BBQ Restaurant in Times Square. The owners thought that it might finally be time to do some traditional marketing, rather than relying solely on great food, great value, and word of mouth, which had been so successful for them up to that point. After discussing our options, we agreed on a media plan that made the most sense for reaching both tourists and New Yorkers.

Once the media choice is made, it always leads to the questions this book is designed to help you answer: What will the message be? There was never a formal creative strategy formulated, but at least because this was a family-owned business, meetings with the owners meant that questions would be answered quickly and decisions would be made promptly.

What could we have said about Dallas BBQ? There were many messages that would have made sense. We could have focused on their:

- ♦ Baby back ribs, specially sourced and especially meaty.
- ♦ Rotisserie chickens, which were always served hot and fresh since they were the largest seller of rotisserie chickens in the city.
- ♦ Low prices that included an early bird special for two people that, at the time, was less than $10 (and in fact, still is).
- ♦ Frozen drinks, featuring Texas-sized versions that were served in 20-ounce glasses.

You know the dilemma; when there is not a strategy, how do you know which creative answer is the correct answer? When I finally developed a good idea and phrase I liked, my concern was that it was not dazzling or creative enough. Yet what I liked about the clarity and positioning of the phrase easily overcame its lack of sparkle. The basis for the idea was that given the number of restaurants they owned and the number of seats in each, they served more BBQ than anyone else in the city. The slogan that flowed from this was "Dallas BBQ. New York's Most Popular BBQ Restaurant."

What it managed to do was avoid having to pick just one of the many distinctly good things the restaurants had to offer (would you have chosen the ribs, the drinks, the value, or the chicken as the basis of your good idea?). Further, strategically it said to people who had already dined there that they had selected wisely; after all, they were eating New York's most popular BBQ. Those who had not yet discovered Dallas BBQ could feel that its popularity gave it credibility and that it was worth seeking out.

Did the phrase "sing?" Would it be the answer when the question was, "And now the award for best creative slogan of the year goes to . . .?" Who cared?

Good Idea: Do you think it is better to focus on one benefit or detail about your Phufkel as the basis of your good idea? Or do you think you will be better served having an all-encompassing theme that speaks to the entire Phufkel experience? Does your Phufkel have one mind-boggling attribute that seems an obvious choice on which to build your campaign and theme? Or should you focus on a different compelling feature in every ad or mailing? They both are reasonable approaches; you will have to make up your own mind.

In the case of Dallas BBQ, the slogan was clear, direct, and six words that in combination with their distinctive logo helped establish them as a true brand separate from any other BBQ-come-lately in New York. For the important Times Square tourist market, which may never have heard of Dallas BBQ, it certainly would now allow the restaurant to be in the consideration set when people were deciding on a place to eat. For diners at any of their restaurants, whether the Times Square location or not, it certainly validated their decision.

One last example of how clear and clever can be one and the same. At one point in my career I worked at the ad agency that had Con Edison, a New York Electric utility company, as an account. The strategy for the campaign was to convince people to leave a light on at night to prevent robberies and break-ins. The campaign theme, "To Stop A Thief, Light A Light," had already been created. (Yes, the campaign was one that would perhaps be considered environmentally incorrect today.)

I came up with a good idea for a television commercial that was about as simple and clear as you could get. Was it also clever? You tell me.

The production company found two identical side-by-side houses to shoot the spot I had created. The camera was locked down facing the front of the houses, so that you saw both houses from the same angle during the entire commercial. It was evening, each house was dark and in shadows, looking slightly ominous except for a light coming from what was obviously the television room of each home. (The art director and I used our own names for the families in the commercial. The names sounded authentic because they really were, and it was as much fun for us to hear our names on television as it would be for you to hear your own name.)

What the viewer saw as the announcer (the actor Jack Klugman, in fact) spoke the voice over were literal renditions of what the announcer was describing.

Announcer: Mr. and Mrs. Heyman turned off the TV (PAUSE AS ROOM IN HOUSE ON LEFT SIDE OF FRAME GETS SLIGHTLY DIM), turned off the light (PAUSE AS ROOM GOES TOTALLY DARK), and went to sleep. Mr. and Mrs. Krivacsy turned off the TV (PAUSE AS ROOM IN HOUSE ON RIGHT SIDE

OF FRAME GETS SLIGHTLY DIM), turned *on* a light
(PAUSE AS ROOM GETS BRIGHT), and went to sleep.
(The viewer is now looking at two houses at night: one
completely dark and in shadow, the other still with a light
on, shining brightly in the dark.) Announcer: If you were
a burglar, which house would you rob? To stop a thief,
light a light.

Simple, visual, dramatic, a clear, clever, good idea!

8

TAKING AN IDEA FROM NICE TO GOOD

As you write down your thoughts, even though you are not yet putting them in any definite order, several ideas will seem better than others. Others may not yet appear particularly good, but you believe there still may be some potential. The challenge is to make the idea as good as you can. The beauty, and one of the characteristics, of a good idea is that it takes on a life of its own.

It is what often happens when you write a short story or a play. Some character that you barely remember creating takes on a more and more important role, and actually starts to dominate the piece. And you sort of just sit back and watch and begin to feel more as if you are taking dictation from the character than creating. (This often happens with actors in television series. They start with a bit part and, thanks to chemistry, talent, and luck, their role gets expanded as the audience indicates it wants to see more of the character.)

That is what happens with a good idea. It does not, however, usually happen with a nice idea or a decent idea. Some ideas you may like initially because they seem comfortable and familiar, which is exactly the reason you should be careful.

I saw this happen early in my career, when we were working on a bear-shaped plastic jelly dispenser. The head of the production department, quite proudly, came up with a name for the product: "Mr. Jelly Belly." What ideas like Mr. Jelly Belly have is that they are nice, obvious, and unnoticed. Yes, it's much better than calling your product "Jelly In A Plastic Bear-Shaped Container." Hmmm, wait, I think I take that back.

What can you do to take an idea from nice to good? You must prod it, poke it, look at it from different angles, and write down your thoughts in unusual ways to see if you can find that unexpected twist that brings it to life.

Good Idea: Find an ad you like, even if it is a competitor's ad. Try to discover exactly what about the ad attracts you. Change a few of the words, one at a time. Find clearer, more precise words, apt synonyms. Figure out the strategy that is captured in the headline, and see how else you could express the thought. See what direction this takes you and follow it as it takes you farther away from the original phrase. Experiment with different sentence breaks to strengthen the message. Move the image in the ad from top to bottom or put it at the side. Use a new picture. Increase the white space. Try larger type. Some of these are merely mechanical changes. Some will lead you to meaningful differences from the original message. But when you get done, you will hopefully have an improved piece of communication.

Naturally Fresh is a division of Eastern Foods, a manufacturer of salad dressings. They gave my agency an assignment to develop trade advertising for a new line of salad dressings they had created. (Trade advertising is directed toward wholesalers or distributors who resell to the public, as opposed to advertising created for the consumer who purchases items).

Historically, trade advertising focuses on some form of "stock, feature, and display": This product will fly off the shelves because it is so well priced or because it tastes so good or because we are supporting it with a massive advertising budget so you should feature it in your circulars, stock enough so that you won't run out of it, and provide at the very least an end aisle display.

The appeal of the product was directed to children, as evidenced by the two product names—Kids' Ranch Outrageous Orange and Purple Pizzazz—with product colors to match. I could have done a nice "Introducing The Most Colorful Salad Dressings Kids Have Ever Seen," or something pleasant enough, such as "The Only Thing More Outrageous Than The Name On The Outside Is How Many Vitamins We've Put Inside." Certainly acceptable, not embarrassing, it would have been good enough, but barely.

Since the client was willing to break the rules of the salad dressing product category, the least I could do was come up with something that at the minimum stretched the rules of trade advertising.

My solution addressed a common concern of super-market owners and managers of produce departments. High on their list of aggravations was a kid wreaking havoc in their stores, touching merchandise, playing with cans, and running around causing general pandemonium. The headline and copy in the ad played directly off that fear. With art direction by Milton Vahue, it featured a big jar of each of the dressings and this headline: "Just What You Need. More Kids Running Around Your Aisles." The body copy quickly reassured the reader that the kids would be running around asking their moms to purchase these new kids' dressings. They would also be running around begging mom to buy carrot sticks, celery, and other veggies because kids love the fun of dipping and drenching all kinds of vegetables into these colorful tasty dressings. There was the reassurance of the product being a great source of vitamins with no artificial preservatives. The copy wraps up at the end saying, "Basically, your concern shouldn't be all the kids running around. Your concern should be not running out."

Good Idea: I do not know where the rule started or even if it is really considered sacrosanct. But when you are writing your body copy, it is a good idea at the end of the body copy to somehow refer back to your headline. Usually it nicely ties everything up, like the dénouement of a story or movie. Is it a rule you can break? Sure. But I usually try to follow it, myself.

CASE HISTORY: LEGION PAPER

Legion Paper sources the finest papermakers around the globe and sells quality printing papers from a variety of manufacturers. One particular product line, Legion Limited Edition Papers, was intended for the publishers and printers of fine art. Artists used these papers because they were archival; that is, the papers would last a long time without deteriorating. For this reason the image would last longer, keeping both the artist and the purchaser of the print very happy.

The client wanted an ad for this, so I did an ad. (It often works that way.)

The ad, art directed by John Twomey, featured a classic image of the Sphinx, with parts of its face eroded through the passage of time, weather, and the environment. The headline was "What Good Is A Long Life If You End Up Looking Old And Worn?" The copy went on to say, among other things, that "these 100% cotton papers will help ensure that their work will stand the test of time thanks to naturally longer fibers, which make the paper stronger and longer lasting. And calcium carbonate buffering acts as a barrier against both the acid in paper and pollutants in the environment."

It was decided that we would send a letter to publishers and printers of fine art posters telling them how superior the papers were. But we wanted something that would make the mailing stand out. Further thinking helped me come up with the idea of sending a roll of Tums with the letter. It was done to suggest to the publisher that we understand deciding which paper to print on is a difficult decision that can lead to an upset stomach so here's an antacid to make you feel better.

This was, at best, a nice idea. The problem was that it was too generic; anyone could use that idea for just about any Phufkel they were selling. That is, anybody could send an antacid anytime they wanted to make the point that selecting the proper "whatever" is tough on your stomach. Or enclose an aspirin and say making a difficult decision can give you a headache.

What turned this into a good idea was using the following (abridged) copy in my letter that accompanied the Tums. The key to the good idea was the portion of the copy I have put into italics for you:

"Selecting the perfect limited edition paper is a difficult decision. Will the paper print well? Is it truly archival? Will the paper deteriorate over time? No wonder your stomach gets all tight, nervous and queasy. Well, just relax, and take one of the enclosed antacids. It will show you why making your Limited Edition Paper decision can be an easy one. *You see, the same ingredient—calcium carbonate—that works so well to neutralize the acid in your stomach is what helps make our papers so durable and long lasting. The calcium carbonate buffering in our papers acts as a barrier against both the acid in paper and pollutants in the environment,* helping to protect the surface of the sheet."

The mailing was very successful, and the client even decided to hand out Tums at their next trade show to remind buyers of their unique message.

The Tums idea was a wonderful example of relevant shock, while the trade show sampling of the Tums was a great example of using the whole carcass. But the major point here is that ultimately you are the one who will have to decide if an idea is just nice or really good. And it is up to you to make it good.

Here's another example. There is a Good restaurant in New York. (Actually, though this sounds like a routine in a Marx brother's movie, "Good" is really the restaurant's name.) While there may have been many fine names they could have settled on for their take-out department, their choice was a good idea: *Good To Go.*

Finally, my networking group took a booth at a small business expo. We wanted to invite people to come as guests to a meeting and see for themselves what an organization that specialized in business referrals was like. We produced a sign and some cards to distribute. The nice idea was to state that being a member was like having 30 salespeople carrying your card and referring your business. What made it a good idea was the twist I put on the cover of the invitation, which acknowledged the skepticism I felt certain was out there: Enjoy a free breakfast with 30 strangers who truly want to help you build your business. (Yeah, we didn't believe it either.)

A nice idea, as I have said, is still better than no idea. It does what it has to do and will get some attention. But think of a good idea as being a nice idea with a microphone in front of it; it will simply be heard by more people, with no extra effort on your part.

9

DON'T TALK SO MUCH

Given the limited attention span of most people, there is rarely any benefit to using long-winded headlines or thoughts—with all the normal caveats and exceptions you are certain to come up with, as I myself do at the end of this chapter.

Occasionally it might work to help you stand out from a field of short headlines. Another reason may be if your thought is too complex for it to be reduced to a few words. (Though I would suggest your premise is probably too complex also and should be simplified.)

No matter what you may have heard, longer is not always better. As Mies van der Roh said, in a very different context, "Less is more."

A popular example of this theory is known as the "elevator pitch." You are supposed to polish your marketing/sales pitch down to a sound bite that could be communicated in the amount of time you would theoretically have during an elevator ride to tell someone about your Phufkel. This is not my favorite analogy for many reasons. What floor are you on when you start? How tall is the building? More important, no one talks in elevators.

I know that you are not really supposed to use this pitch only on elevators ("Sorry, I can't tell you about my Phufkel just yet, we are only in the lobby. Wait till we get into the elevator."). But it is a helpful technique in learning to compress your marketing message.

I prefer to think about it this way: Imagine having to create an idea for an out-of-home billboard seen only by those driving past it at 55 miles per hour. To make it even more interesting, pretend that there are several billboards to the right and left of yours competing for the same attention as yours. Now the test: What are the fewest words you can put your message into and still attract attention to your idea?

This has nothing to do with the ingenuity of the words. I assume you will make them dazzling. But all things being equal, the fewer words you can use to convey your idea while still keeping the voice, the uniqueness, and the essence, that is all to the good.

Another challenge I like, similar to the billboard test, is the traveling salesman experiment. No, not the one about the farmer's daughter. This is the one where you are a traveling salesman. You knock on a door and, when it is answered, you have five seconds to get your prospect's attention. How many words do you think you will be able to speak before you get the door slammed in your face? It is not like a business meeting, or life, where you can ramble a little. This is the moment of truth for your message.

You may think what you have to say is so captivating and persuasive that you can use a longer message to get and keep people's attention. Perhaps indeed you can. I am sure a large percentage of the people who create messages believe that their Phufkel and their message are exceptionally interesting. But just as the children in the town of Lake Wobegon can not really all be above average, consider the possibility that your message is not provocative enough to get people to spend the time it takes to settle in with it.

When it comes to body copy, as opposed to the headline or slogan, brevity is even more desirable. While this does not mean all your sentences should be kept to a minimum, it does mean that you should not write more than you have to and certainly not more that your audience has any interest in reading. You want to pique the reader's interest, not satisfy it. If you tell them everything you know about your Phufkel in your ad, aside from probably being too wordy and therefore uninteresting, it is more than they need or want to know at this stage. Be sure to leave something on the table for the sales call or the follow up. You should not make it too complicated or pack too much information into the page. Resist the temptation to show off your deep understanding of Phufkels in general and yours in particular by quoting chapter, verse, and anecdotes. There is a place for a lengthy copy, but unless you are a really excellent writer it is awfully difficult to pull off. Direct mail, which often calls for an immediate reaction and response, can take the liberty of using copious copy. Ads for luxury items can use long copy, offering reasons that help consumers rationally justify an emotional decision to spend a lot of money. Long copy, in general, is problematic because people just haven't the time or desire to read it all. While we all know the impact the Declaration of Independence has had on our lives, you can probably only quote the first line, or recognize a few of the opening phrases ("When, in the course of human events . . . We hold these truths to be self-evident, that all men are created equal, that they are endowed by their Creator with certain unalienable rights, that among these are life, liberty and the pursuit of happiness."). But few of us have any idea of what else is in there, such as the listing of the actual grievances against the king. It just seems to go on and on.

(Is it a) Good Idea? Are you aware of the John Hancock ad the John Hancock Company runs every Independence Day? It is a full-page reproduction of the actual Declaration of Independence, without any of the usual attributions, such as "this page has been brought to you by." The assumption is that the large John Hancock signature at the center of the signatures on the bottom is enough to make people aware of whom the page is sponsored by. I assume they send out copies to newspapers and schools to make certain they get their full share of PR. But what do you think? Did you know about this? Have they been doing it too long? Would you do it if it were your company? How subtle do you think you can you be and still be effective?

A Holiday Story

The annual holiday card. Everyone sends them. Some are stunning. Some are hokey. Even the best examples are displayed for a short while, then, while much appreciated, discarded and forgotten. Don't think that's true? Okay. Name a few cards you received this year. (Don't feel badly if you can't. Most people probably can't recall last year's Academy Award winner for best actor either.) There is, however, always an opportunity to do something more, something that stands out from the common card. (Of course, you have to be respectful of the sensitivity of your audience to their holiday season, but that is a challenge, not a limitation.)

Several years ago my agency did a mailing in an attempt to acquire some new clients. It was a traditional approach. We purchased a mailing list, based on zip codes, SIC codes, number of employees, and years in business. Then we mailed two letters several weeks apart extolling, in lengthy, detailed prose, the merits of Porte Advertising, who we were, and why they might care. We followed up with phone calls. We did all the "right things." And the result was . . . zilch!

Did we give up and feel depressed and despondent? Of course we did. After all, we were in the business of being clever and making people pay attention to our efforts. And we had struck out. However (and let us be thankful for all the "howevers" of the world), I decided to try once more. It was getting close to the holiday season, and I sent out some oversize postcards with the following message as the only words on the page: In The Spirit Of The Season, We Feel It Is Only Right To Let You Know We Have Also Been Sending Our Mailings To Your Competition.

Surprising for a holiday message? No doubt. But it was also relevant, unexpected, a little gutsy, and effective. We received a phone call from one of the recipients, and his company eventually hired us. (Turns out he had no recollection of any of our other mailings, which made perfect sense as they were, in hindsight, absolutely, completely, perfectly, unacceptably ordinary.)

Certainly that is not an example of a short headline, but when I suggest not talking so much I do not only or necessarily mean the headline. In this case, though, the headline was more than 25 words, it was the only text on the page, had lots of space around it, was very easy and inviting to read, along with being, as we had hoped, provocative.

 Good Idea: Are you doing a mailing to your clients? Of course you are. At the very least, aren't you sending them invoices, price lists, press releases, news about your company or Phufkel, or advertising reprints? Use these opportunities, since you are making contact anyway, to do something unexpected. Don't save your good ideas only for what

you consider important projects. The good idea
I had was not the idea of sending the postcard for
the holiday card; that was just the mechanics. The
good idea was the message. So while you may use
a different color, size, or shape, which will help you
to stand out, the actual message—the idea—is
more important.

CASE HISTORY: PARADIGM VISION VIDEO CONFERENCING

WinTel Communications Corporation, based in New York,
provides telecommunications products and services. They
install, administer, maintain, provide billing, and in general
do everything required to keep phone systems working.
Our project was to create a brand identity (slogan, logo,
sales sheet, business cards, press release, a DVD, sales kit,
trade show booth) for a new web-enabled video conferencing capability, one with exceptional clarity and port-
ability. You could literally remotely zoom in and read the
date on a dime in the corner of a room. Since it did not
require a dedicated video conferencing room, you could
communicate from anywhere in the world with a broadband connection, telephone, and a computer. Along with
that, the software had a host of special features: desktop
applications such as PowerPoint could be inserted into
meetings, an archival business library could be established so users could utilize previously stored histori-
cal files and videos, participants could store, create, and
forward e-mail and also capture anything the camera was
seeing, such as charts, graphs, and exhibits, for their own
use later. We named this the Focus Video Conferencing
System.

Also important to the idea generating process: a lurking deadline. The company had committed to renting a booth at a major trade show that was just a few months away. So on day one of our discussions we had that all-too-familiar blank page, along with a fixed, rapidly approaching cut-off date for the creation, execution, and production of all the elements they required. Or, failing that, signage at their booth that said only, "Compliments of a friend."

Good Idea: When you are faced with a deadline, and you always will be, spend time at the beginning figuring out all your alternate plans for when things don't go as well as you had hoped because they never will. It will snow in July, the flight will be cancelled, the brochure won't dry, there will be a sudden strike, the specs will change, or all of the above. If you are placing an ad, speak to the rep or directly to the publisher to find out the actual date they require materials; often they will then give you a considerable amount of extended time, because the original due date was for their safety and comfort, not yours. Also, just as publications will not always be totally straightforward about their actual closing dates, perhaps you can, as necessary, be a touch less than candid to your sources with the due dates you give them to provide some breathing room in your schedule. (You can't successfully do this more than once or twice to retain any credibility, so save it for special occasions.)

For Focus Video Conferencing, the slogan we ultimately used was "It's Better Than Being There." Only five words, so it was certainly short enough. The reason I liked it as a good idea was because of the layers of meaning it contained. It didn't matter how many of those meanings were clear at first; the fuller meaning of the line could be explained in ads, brochures, other marketing communications, in person, or video conferences.

On one level, "Better Than Being There" referred to the businessman being able to avoid the hassle, expense, and long security lines at airports associated with travel. On that level alone it made legitimate sense. But there were other meanings as well, referring to the capabilities of the system. When you attend a meeting in person and you need to reference a file you have archived or installed in a computer that you don't have with you, well, too bad. But with Focus, you can retrieve the info you need on your computer and share it with other conference members who can save the information to their own machines. You don't have to worry about finding a dedicated videoconference room in whatever country or hotel you are in. A telephone and a broadband connection for your computer is all that is required.

This is what led me to the other good idea, the two-word good idea. Given the specific capabilities of the Focus System and the target audience (obviously business people; consumers did not need the high resolution quality, price, and range of services Focus was capable of), I created a new category, of which Focus was proudly the first and only member. The category was Business Optimized Video Conferencing, the two key words being *"Business Optimized."* At last, a video conferencing system designed and created for the businessman, not the family that wants to keep video contact with distant family members or far-off college students.

In just two words a new category of video conferencing had been created!

You are going to look over all the ideas you have created and truncate them, because you are now convinced that the fewer the words the better. While generally true, the directive is that it is not always the number of words, but rather the clarity of the words. JPMorganChase, or whatever their current name is, used a slogan: "Your choice. Your Chase." Four words. But they should have used a few more. I have no idea what they are trying to say. Sometimes I feel as if I do, but then the meaning fades away before it starts making real sense. Once I thought "Your Choice" meant they realize you can bank with many other institutions. But then they add "Your Chase," which seems to say that they are currently my bank, which they are not. And who in real life spends this much time trying to decipher a slogan?

So the real lesson is that a headline, slogan, or text should be as long as it should be, but not a word longer.

10

RELEVANT SHOCK

It's no surprise that everyone likes a surprise. Well, perhaps people only enjoy a pleasant surprise. But pleasant or not there is still something about a shocker that makes us pay attention.

It is easy to attract attention with a graphic or combination of words. If you just want to invite attention, just do something really outrageous. How about a nice juicy profanity, splashed across the center of the page in a vibrant contrasting color from the rest of the message? Do you have one selected? Go ahead, put it down. Feel good about it? Fine. But there is one problem, which you may have anticipated. While it may prove easy to get someone's attention this way, what actual good does it do you? If it has nothing to do with what you are trying to accomplish, what does it matter if people read your headline? Obviously only a segment of the world out there has any interest in your Phufkels to begin with. So attracting the attention of someone who has no need for a Phufkel will not be very beneficial in your quest to sell more of them. You are not interested in how large an audience you reach with your message. You are more interested in reaching the audience who might use your product or service. Getting a bald man to look at your ad for a hairbrush because you have gotten his attention will not do you much good. And a nice juicy curse word won't really help your business, unless your Phufkels are unabridged dictionaries. While it is easy to get people to look at your message, if the message has no relevance to what you are selling, the reader will leave even more quickly than he arrived.

The element of surprise is the very least you can put into the execution of an idea and expect it to be noticed. You want to be surprising and unique and innovative.

It's just that you have to realize that that is only half the battle. Just as importantly, you must combine your shock with relevance. There must be a tie-in that flows naturally from your attention-getting surprise to your product and its benefits.

The example I use to illustrate this point is Santa Claus. If you were to see Santa Claus in his red costume and white beard in December, it would be relevant to the season, but not particularly surprising. Yet if you were to spot Santa Claus on the beach in July, in his typical holiday attire, while it would be shocking, it would lack relevance. It doesn't connect with anything. Ideally, your message must combine surprise, to get the piece noticed, and relevance, so that there is a connection between the surprise and your message.

Try to find a provocative thought for your headline relevant to your Phufkel, the category, and your target. Avoid safe, familiar, lackluster words. They are, unfortunately, easy to create and, just as unfortunately, easily overlooked. *If you think you have heard it before, you have.*

Remember, it is not the medium that determines how hard you work to find the relevant shock. Recently I was in a men's room, standing at the urinal. On the wall facing me was an ad for an online Internet gambling site with this headline: Stop Playing With Yourself. It was a relevant and shocking thought, considering where I was and how I was occupied at the moment. If it weren't trying to convince me to join an online group, it wouldn't have been relevant to anything, merely an invasive admonishment. But given the setting, it was quite effective. I don't think whoever created it said, "Why bother coming up with a good idea, it is only going to be seen in bathrooms."

Good Idea: If you don't have a sense of humor, get one. For the most part, the communications that get remembered, become part of the American culture, and attain a longer than average life, have off-beat senses of humor to them. You don't have to make the reader guffaw. A smile, a chuckle, a head nod of recognition can do it. Humor is often a good means of implanting your message, though admittedly even more subjective than people's ideas of beauty. After all, on every list of attributes that a prospective mate looks for, the top three always include a sense of humor. While drama, logic, empathy, and emotion can work well, especially in financial or luxury goods categories or in long-copy direct marketing pieces, it is often more difficult to do it convincingly.

The reason humor often works in advertising and marketing is that by and large it relies on a different way of looking at things, a caption or punch line or juxtaposition that is unexpected, but comes naturally out of the set up. Hmmm, sounds like what you should be doing with your communications, doesn't it?

The opposite of relevant shock is "borrowed interest." I am mentioning it only in the same way I would mention a rattlesnake; it is something to avoid. Basically, borrowed interest is when you take the drama that is inherent in something and try to link it, no matter how illogically, to your Phufkel. Sometimes this becomes the "Just as, so too" school of advertising. (*Just as* this spaceman can jump 300 feet in the air, *so too* can you jump higher when you wear these sneakers.)

I have been guilty of this, my only excuse being I was young and wanted an expense-paid trip to Florida. We went to shoot a series of gasoline commercials that were built around a set of tips on saving fuel. This particular spot opened on a beautiful girl in a bikini who was holding a beach ball. She tossed it to the spokesman, who said something like, "This beach ball can show you how to save gasoline." He squeezed it, to show that it was not fully inflated, making the analogy that *just as* this beach ball won't bounce as well with less air, *so too* your tires will burn more gas if they are not inflated properly. While the analogy was indeed accurate, we certainly didn't really require the girl in the bikini on the beach to make the point. It's a perfect example of borrowed interest. While I was one of the many who never complained about it, unless you can get a free trip to Florida and have lunch with a beautiful person in a skimpy bathing suit, please try to stick with relevant shock.

CASE HISTORY: FRIGIDAIRE WASHING MACHINES

Frigidaire washing machines once had as a point of difference: a "deep action agitator." The claim was that the deep action agitator would help to truly deep clean clothing, but in a gentle manner. My challenge was to prove this. Normally this might lead you to some sort of demonstration. What I didn't want to do was a typical side-by-side demonstration, with the usual end result that one pile of clothing looked, well, more deeply cleaned than a competitor's. But I did want to show how effective this unusual agitator really was. Here's what I came up with, and to the client's credit, it was approved and aired.

We opened on a shot of a young boy, a wooden stool and a clear plastic full-sized mock-up of the washing machine. It was transparent so that we could see the actual action of the agitator during the commercial. There was also his high-sided, handmade wooden wagon. On the side of the wagon was printed, in a kid's handwriting, "Frigidaire Deep Action Agitator Demonstration." As the announcer spoke, the child took a metal container from the wagon and poured the white liquid contents into the washing machine, which was then turned on so we could see the agitator and the power currents it created. He then added a chocolate colored liquid from a glass jar and finally—but how could it be—what appeared to be a few scoops of vanilla ice cream. In synch with his actions, and using appropriate close ups, the announcer stated, "A demonstration of the deep action agitator of the Frigidaire Jet-Action washer. The agitator that gently deep cleans clothes with power currents like these. The deep action agitator of the Frigidaire Jet-Action washer gently deep cleans clothes. . . ." At this point we cut away from the close ups of the contents of the washer and the currents to see the boy sitting on the stool with a long large straw as he eagerly drinks from the washing machine. And the announcer confesses, "And it makes a wild milk-shake too!"

We then cut to the slogan and logo, as we heard a sound effect of the slurping of a straw while he finished the milkshake.

Was this an example of a good idea? After all, there wasn't a clean item of clothing to be seen anywhere, and isn't that we really wanted to prove?

However, it clearly demonstrated the claim of deep action agitation and gentleness, along with demonstrating a certain casual confidence on the part of the manufacturer. It was just as enjoyable on repeated viewings—certainly to me—even though there was no longer a surprise payoff.

Certainly it was relevant and surprising. A good idea indeed.

 Good Idea: Consider a demonstration of a unique quality or improvement or modification of your Phufkel as the basis for a good idea. You could compare your "new" Phufkel to your old Phufkel (newly improved) or your competitor's Phufkel. But attempt to avoid a cliché demo; side-by-side is often simply not unusual enough. If your Phufkel now does its job faster, easier, more economically, less noisily, with a feature never offered before, don't just tell your customers about it; if you can, show them. If you can't show them, then perhaps come up with a better good idea than a demonstration.

CASE HISTORY: THE AMERICAN ARBITRATION ASSOCIATION

This organization, as it defines itself, "provides services to individuals and organizations that wish to resolve conflicts out of court." Most people think of it as offering binding arbitration or alternative dispute resolution, including mediation.

When I worked on their business, it quickly became clear that they were an organization run by people who took their responsibilities very seriously, as is fitting for an association dealing with important legal issues. This did not mean that they were not warm, friendly people with a sense of humor. They were. But it did mean that Denny Crane, from *Boston Legal*, would not have made partner.

What I got out of the meetings and briefings was that they considered themselves an alternative to the court case system and trials where people fought to the end, made enemies, and were basically adversarial. There were many good ideas I presented, but only one really stood out as far as I was concerned. Fortunately, and somewhat surprisingly to me, the client agreed. (I have noticed that I am frequently surprised when a client selects the best idea. I am not sure if that is because I do not give them enough credit in the first place, the idea is not as radical as I believe it is so there is no real danger in selecting it, or if it is simply that most people have the ability to spot a good idea even if hidden in a pile of otherwise ordinary thoughts.)

The thought that triggered my idea was that the Association didn't think it was either right or necessary to turn an adversary into an enemy. You could, they believed, have a settlement to an issue that helped preserve—not harm—a business relationship. This led me to my good idea, which while it did not invoke the Ten Commandments, certainly invoked another significant authority: mothers.

On the center of the page near the top was a long, wide gray column bordered in black. It contained a group of quotes: "Don't fight," "Be Fair," "Try To Work Things Out," "Listen To The Other Person."

The headline was below the box of quotes and explained the origin of these rules and attitudes: "Don't Forget What Your Mother Always Told You."

Text next to the quotations said that basic common sense is the whole idea behind the American Arbitration Association's alternative dispute resolution procedures. It explained that it is not necessary to turn an adversary into an enemy and went on to talk about its advantages over traditional litigation. All of it was based on the advice that mothers gave to their children, including those who grew up to become lawyers.

You can imagine how out of the ordinary an ad like this looked in a somber publication such as "American Lawyer" and other legal profession magazines. It was formal in design, dignified in its appeal, and appropriate to the audience. But it also was certainly surprising.

I remember hearing about a writer who, when he got an assignment, would write down every expected cliché element in the category. If the assignment was to create a dog food commercial, he would write on his list dogs, dog bowls, smiling kids, and beaming moms. Then he would do his darndest to keep those items out of his commercials to make sure they would look as different from the category norm as possible. Even though he probably never completely succeeded, he did at least stand a better chance of his commercials being good ideas than those who rushed right into the arms of the clichés of the category. (Do not attempt this at home. He was a trained professional and did not make his list just for the sake of being different. Nor should you.)

I must admit, however, that it is getting harder and harder to astonish anyone. The images you see in the movies, on network television, cable stations, and most noticeably online are close to eliminating the need for an active imagination. The language you hear on radio and television, from actors and politicians, would have gotten many mouths washed out with soap not too long ago. Yet the piece you have created—the ad, sign, commercial, or brochure—will not work if it is not noticed or if it is dull, expected, or boring. But if it is provocative solely for the sake of shock—with no relevant payoff—it will not be effective.

11

LOST YOUR VOICE?

Every person has his or her own voice. It is a combination of the pacing, accent, pitch, tone, vocabulary, and inflection. Put them all together and you have a distinctive voice and unique sound.

It is the same with your communications. You want to create a good idea for your Phufkel, to make it seem singular and desirable. The sound should reflect the identity you have created. I don't mean "sound" only as in the sound that comes from your iPod or television. The printed word also has a sound of its own. It is the unique voice of your Phufkel and one that you need to capture in every message you create.

Here is what I mean: Read the following paragraph out loud, in the style of Woody Allen or Clint Eastwood, or Whoopi Goldberg.

"Breakfast at the Stage Deli is not chopped liver. It is portions you cannot finish without you have an assistant. There are deli omelettes which it will take two of you to lift from the plate, on account of their being overstuffed with corned beef, pastrami or salami. Smoked fish platters from which you can decide on your preference of nova, belly lox, white fish, baked salmon, and sturgeon. The Stage cheese blintzes, which are in the category of best in the city, are presented with sour cream and preserves of fruit. We serve breakfast all day, from whenever you arise to whenever shuteye is deemed necessary. Or, if you do not wish to turn up here, there are eager delivery persons who are accessible from 7:00 A.M. to midnight. Enjoy breakfast at the Stage—especially if you are not planning on eating for the rest of the day."

It doesn't flow does it? Doesn't make sense. It just doesn't seem fitting.

Now read the same passage again, but read it as if you were a character in *Guys and Dolls* or any story by Damon Runyon or using the voice of any cliché New York tough guy.

Works a lot better, doesn't it? Because that's the voice the paragraph is written in; though it is at best a pale imitation of Mr. Runyon, it is a voice appropriate for the message. It is possible you never had a specific voice that you used for your Phufkel. Or maybe you once had a voice, but you have experimented with strategies so frequently and have changed direction so often that you have lost your original identity. But you really need to find your voice and once you have found it, never let it go.

CASE HISTORY: THE STAGE DELI

The breakfast passage you just read is based on signage I created for New York's Stage Deli, which has been a Broadway hangout since it opened in 1937. It is famous for its overstuffed sandwiches and as a home for cheerful celebrities and grumpy waiters. It is still filled day and night with Broadway characters, both sitting at the tables and waiting on the tables.

The short section you read is written in a more overdone style than the original window sign, to make a point. But you can see how important it is to give the proper voice to whatever words you are writing; it makes your text more distinctive, more fitting, and more convincing.

The signage we did for the Stage Deli was very important to help maintain its special voice. The restaurant's long stretch of window space directly on Seventh Avenue is a very valuable piece of real estate, with wonderful possibilities for appropriate, timely messages. Used properly, it helps to create a feeling of "I am entering a legendary New York deli and it's going to be a great experience."

The marketing we did for the Stage always included a strategy beyond being simply creative, just as yours should. But the expression of that strategy was always filtered through the personality and reputation of the restaurant. What was the reputation? How about grumpy, but entertaining waiters, huge portions, sandwiches named after celebrities, and unfortunately, sandwiches that were not regarded as particularly inexpensive. The last point, the pricing, was one of the more important strategic issues. How do you convince a tourist that a sandwich at the Stage Deli was worth $14 or $15 or more? For all I knew that amount of money could provide a meal for four in the tourist's hometown. If the strategy was to convince a vacationer that even though it might appear pricey they got more than their money's worth at the Stage, it had to be expressed in a way that was appropriate to the "voice" of the restaurant. Here are four examples of how we accomplished this, each art directed by Milton Vahue.

In a print ad, we crammed a close-up picture of a Stage triple-decker overflowing with corned beef, pastrami, coleslaw, and cheese. It filled the entire space on the left half of the ad, from the top to the bottom. To the right of the sandwich, in large type, was the headline: "NO ONE GOES BACK HOME BRAGGING THEY HAD A NICE CHOPPED SALAD." There was no other body copy. We believed that the message would easily be understood. That is, that a customer could go eat at some ordinary restaurant with normal-sized portions of rather ordinary food. Or they could have a once-in-a-vacation food experience that they would remember and talk about when they returned from their visit to New York.

Another ad had a picture of a huge triple-decker sandwich, spilling over with meat and cheese, in the center of the page. The message again was short, simple, and very Stage-y, talking directly to the heft of the sandwich: "REMINDER: PLEASE BEND KNEES WHEN LIFTING."

There was the window sign which simply said, "IF YOU ARE HAVING LUNCH AT THE STAGE DELI, MAY WE SUGGEST YOU CANCEL YOUR RESERVATIONS FOR DINNER."

Lastly, I did a parody of food eating competitions. These are the contests to see who can consume the largest amounts of foods like hot dogs and pizza. Our version had a giant, mouth-watering picture of a huge triple-decker. Above the sandwich was the headline: "The Winner Of The Stage Deli Eating Contest Was Mr. Alvin Gottleib." Then, below the humongous sandwich, was the payoff: "He Actually Finished One!"

What do all these ideas have in common? They all come out of the same strategy (a value—look what you get for your money—strategy) and all are expressed in a tone, attitude, and voice that is pure Stage. They each also had multiple lives, as discussed in the next chapter, "Use The Whole Carcass." The ads became window signs, the window signs became ads, all were the basis for press releases, and everything went on the website.

If the voice of your Phufkel is not an unusual one, don't be concerned. As long as it is clear and consistent with your idea, it will be fine. Simple is better than complex; clear is better than confusing. If your idea does not lend itself or call out for a really distinctive voice, don't force it. Just make certain the tone is consistent with the message and the audience. If you are selling highly technical Phufkels, then let your tone be consistent with that.

Good Idea: A fun experiment. If your Phufkel were a person, who would it be? How about if it were a movie star? Which actor is your Phufkel most like? Male? Female? Action hero or intellectual? American or foreign? Young? Old? When you think this through and come up with an answer, you will have a better idea of the "voice" of your Phufkel. You will better understand its character, temperament, attitude, and most important, its personality. That is what a brand identity is: the product's personality, the ways in which it is distinct, different, and immediately identifiable.

Years ago I created a campaign for Burgermeister (Burgie) beer, from Hamms. Burgie was brewed in California, and its claim was that it was original California beer. The assignment was to develop a campaign to introduce Burgie beer into the Chicago market. My idea was to demonstrate that in some interesting lifestyle aspects, there were surprising parallels between Californians and Chicagoans. One commercial featured the windsurfing that both did on their respective bodies of water. Though one was on an ocean, one on a lake, they both enjoyed the same lively sport. The slogan brought that concept into words with the thought that "If you live our life, you're gonna love our beer."

Art director Ray Krivacsy and I went to Chicago and California to shoot the spots. The creative director was to join us after we had cast the talent and scouted the locations. When our boss showed up he immediately told us that he had changed the copy at the beginning of the spot and that the client had agreed to his changes. When he told me what the changes were, I was particularly annoyed because it was clear that he was right.

What he had done was to eliminate the copy in the start of the spot and replace it with a chorus that was sung over the action of the windsurfers. The lyrics were simply "Burgie, original California, California beer." It sounded great and was marvelously appropriate for the commercial and the target audience of young adults. The words I had written, logical, rational and perhaps even leaning towards persuasive, were simply the wrong voice for the beer category in general and wrong in tone in particular for a commercial using an emotional lifestyle sell.

Since by now you are probably just as eager or even more delighted to learn from my missteps as from my successes, here's another example of my using the wrong voice for a project.

A synagogue I belonged to was starting a fund-raising effort, and I was on the publicity committee. They had named the campaign "Fund for the Future" and already had a theme for the project. The goal was to raise enough money to enlarge and modernize the space in the Temple, as we were running out of room for our members and seating was getting cramped. My assignment was to create some thoughts to use as the basis for a mailing to members of the congregation. When I presented the ideas to the committee and the Rabbi, I could tell that, though I was going for relevant shock as I usually do, the "shock" element far outweighed the "relevant" component in their eyes. The ideas started from the possibly predictable, "Without your help, we haven't got a prayer" or "We've gotten too small for your britches." They then expanded to "You know how they always say, 'It doesn't matter how much you give, as long as you give'? Well, this time it matters." and "You can't buy your way into heaven. But we would be delighted to put in a good word." Then it was on to the even more irreverent, "A new, expanded, more spacious Temple? Our prayers have been answered." Finally, the last creative straw, "We're running out of space so quickly, we only have room for eight of the ten commandments."

While I had realized that perhaps these went too far, I thought that they could lead to safer versions that would still have some sparkle and stand out from the more expected fund-raising communications. Not a chance. The voice I used was simply not a serious enough tone for a religious institution, especially one that was relying on the message to open wallets of elderly, probably more conservative members. In hindsight, I am glad I wasn't smote during my presentation.

A voice need not actually be present in the words you write. The voice can also be established in your premise. Your idea or concept must be consistent with who you are or who your customers think you are. That's why the strategy is so important. Can you imagine if McDonald's started claiming some version of "Expensive, but worth it"? After going "Huh?" you would probably go straight to Burger King. Don't let your "voice" create a disconnect between your strategy, your idea, and the actual image and individuality of your Phufkel.

USE THE WHOLE CARCASS

Congratulations. You came up with a good idea. You liked it, developed it, and actually used it. Of course, I've no clue as to what your idea was or what you did with it. But at least I am confident you actually had a good idea. (Unless you skipped ahead to this chapter first, because you were intrigued by its title. Well, go back. Now!)

There you are with your idea. You are proud and eager to find another good idea now that you know you can do it. Don't! At least, don't do it yet because there is so much more you can do with your original idea. And it is all those additional uses you should look for that makes the original effort to find the good idea so worthwhile. It is the increased value you will be able to get out of your idea and the many ways you can use it that hopefully you will now start to think about every time you get an idea.

Here's what I mean by use the whole carcass. Thousands of centuries ago when someone was hungry he killed an animal, put it over a fire, ate it, and it was good. But that was just the tasty part. Then he took the skin and made a coat for protection and a blanket for warmth. Then he made the horns into weapons. The bones were ground up for medicine. The sinews used for string. Lots of yucky parts were put to various uses. Point is everything was used, nothing was wasted. I am certain the smart ones looked for even more additional ways to use up every last bit of the beast. (Though I personally do not want to know about the eyeballs.)

Since you are one of the smart ones, you want to do the same with your idea.

You don't have to do this as part of a formal program, but you should always be thinking of what else could be done with your idea. You should examine where else you can use the material you have produced that will make it more marketing effective as well as cost-effective. With each additional use, the less costly it becomes for you to have created it in the first place. Think of it as that large wooly mammoth you have just slaughtered; it was difficult enough to prevail over the creature, you certainly don't want to waste even a morsel.

It may be that this is basic stuff to you. You automatically use the whole carcass, though you never referred to it with that particular phrase. But recently I came across some smart business people who completely overlooked the benefit of making the publicity they were fortunate to receive work even harder for them. One proudly showed us her press book. It was wonderful. She had gotten mentions, quotes, and pictures of her work in a wide range of industry specific, general interest, and relevant trade publications. When I asked her what she did with the articles, she gestured to her impressive black-covered, plastic-sheeted press book. "I always quickly put them into this book," she said.

"And?" I prompted. "And?" she repeated.

"Well, why aren't copies blown up and framed on your wall? Did you send any copies out to your current clients and prospects? Do you have a page on your website dedicated to all this wonderful publicity? Have you. . ."

She was smart. She got it right away. She admitted that it wasn't because she was too busy or that she had no one on staff to take care of that. She had simply never thought of doing that.

Let's say you just created your first ad. Good for you. But don't just sit there, while you gaze adoringly at it, and wonder why the phones haven't begun ringing. While you are waiting, how about seeing if the publication will provide you with reprints. Make some copies yourself, if the publication will allow it. Be certain to eliminate the date—white it out or whatever—because nothing dates a piece quicker than someone seeing it is as old news. Things become old news very quickly, which is a good reason to immediately do the following:

Good Idea:

Good Idea!

- Laminate a copy, so it will not yellow and will always appear fresh
- Send a copy to your clients
- Send a copy to your prospects
- Send a copy to your mother (Trust me on this one.)
- Display a copy, blown up if necessary, in your window, on your wall, on your desk, or all of above.
- Send a copy, with a little PR piece, to your local media outlets (Yes, all of them.)
- Put it on your website

Take something as modest as a flier. You will have to get it printed, but how many copies should you produce? Probably twice as many as you think. Because you do not want to just use them for a mailing or whatever you envisioned as the primary use. They can also be used as handouts near your location, sent to local publications, and sent to existing clients. Naturally it all depends on the piece you have created, but the point is that you should almost always produce extras, because they cost very little more to print. A four-color brochure might cost $3 each if you print 1,000, but the next 1,000 might each cost only $1 once the piece is on the press. At that point, it is really just the paper and ink you are paying for, not the creative development, writing, art direction, or prepress. The incremental printing cost is nil.

If your finished piece is smaller than the page you are printing, think of ways to use the extra space on the page. You are paying for that full page anyway, why just discard the trim? How about using it for a note pad, a bookmark or a phone pad with your name on it?

You should really get in the habit of figuring out what other uses you can get from your idea. This way of thinking will become second nature to you as you go on to develop more and better ideas. Milk it for all it's worth, and it will be worth a lot more. You have struggled to get the idea, make it pay off for you in every way possible.

Here's a starter list of some media and tools that will help ensure that you don't forget about using everything you can to get added value from your idea. This does not mean you have to use them all, but you should be aware of them—the most traditional as well as the latest technological media—as outlets for spreading the good word about your Phufkel. Remember when I told you it was worth working really hard to come up with your good idea, because once you did the rest would be (relatively) easy? You struggled and came up with your good idea and now have the opportunity of using it—or some adaptation of it—on any or all of these:

♦ **Your Business Card:** This is often the first marketing piece that people will see. Never thought of it as a marketing piece? Well, I may be stretching a point, but it has your identity on it and it does represent you and your Phufkel. Just as you wouldn't hand out a smudged, dog-eared card rife with typos to represent you, so too should you really, really think about the appearance of your card— fonts, colors, size, shape—and what it says. Will your good idea—logo, slogan—work in some form on your card?

♦ **Your Brochure:** Do you have or need one? These come in unlimited shapes and sizes, folds and weights, glossy, matte, or laminated finishes. If you don't know your 100 lb Gloss Cover from your 100 lb Gloss Book or your 14 pt Gloss Cover, then find a printer you feel comfortable with, locally or online.

♦ **Your Video:** If your good idea is a commercial or video brochure or sales training piece, then think about using it on your website or adapting it to make it entertaining enough for you to post on video-sharing websites like YouTube.

♦ **Your Press Release.** It certainly isn't very expensive to use a press release to tell the world about your good idea. That's one reason to send your release—mailed, faxed, or e-mailed—to newspapers, magazines, local cable and national television and radio stations, relevant organizations, trade journals, everyone you can think of. Come up with a good idea for your release, one that makes it stand out. If your release is good enough to catch someone's eye and actually be used, you will have the opportunity to have your Phufkel mentioned to thousands of people. One piece of practical advice: Do not bury your lead. This is newspaper talk for cautioning a reporter to get to the point and not hide the most important piece of information three or four paragraphs down while they are busy dramatically setting a scene or building tension. An attention span, like life, is short.

♦ **Your Trade Show.** If your industry has trade shows, only you will know if it is worth the expense to participate. But if you do get a booth, at the very least, in some manner, be certain to utilize everything you have already produced. Display your fliers, brochures, ads, releases, everything. Your brand new slogan, if that has been your good idea, should be prominently displayed. Another good idea is figuring out a way to increase traffic at your booth, without relying on cheap branded giveaways that only attract people who want to add to their dusty collection of cheap branded giveaways. Do not confuse building a brand with putting your brand name on a pen.

♦ **Your Website or Blog.** Today a website is as necessary as a business card. Make certain yours properly reflects the identity you developed for your Phufkel in look and tone. (Find your voice.) Avoid starting a site and then losing your enthusiasm, so that people who come to your site are greeted by an "under construction" notice for months at a time. Equally bad is trying to save money by having your second cousin who took a one-semester computer course design your site. While you do not have to spend a fortune, try not to make it a family affair. (Save your cousin for developing the family genealogy site.) Along with, or instead of, an elaborate site, perhaps a blog would be a good idea.

♦ **Direct Marketing.** You have your good idea. You have your flier, brochure, press release, advertisement. You have your target audience. Think about doing a mailing. It can consist of using materials you already have or adapting the ideas to a different format. This can get very expensive; you probably won't be able to send it to everyone. A mailing list specialist can give you good direction.

♦ **Snarkletv.org:** Actually, there is no such product yet or perhaps ever. Let it represent whatever is the latest communication or networking tool available. Newer than mash-ups, podcasts, wikis, sock puppets, viral marketing, tagging, and RSS feeds. To the extent you are comfortable using the newest gizmo out there, see if it will help you get your message out.

As the saying goes, if your only tool is a hammer, you tend to see every problem as a nail. If you have only a website or a brochure, you will tend to try to fit everything you have into those formats, ignoring the many other marketing communication possibilities that you should take advantage of all the time.

CASE HISTORY: CLEARVISION OPTICAL

I first became aware of the concept of using the whole carcass as a mechanism to bring additional value to a good idea when I saw it used by Peter Friedfeld of ClearVision Optical. ClearVision is a global distributor of prescription, fashion, lifestyle, and children's eyewear frames and at one time was a client of Porte Advertising. (I created their slogan, "It's Easier When You Have A ClearVision," but that story is for a different book.) What Peter did may be common practice in his industry and perhaps scores of others. I had never seen it used so naturally and matter-of-factly. It was as natural for him to use the entire beast as it is for you to automatically order ink when the toner is low. It was part of the checklist, just something you did. Here's one example of how Peter did it with a line of eyewear called Flexit. Flexit's most important difference was that it had an advanced spring hinge. (A spring hinge is a hinge on each side of the frame that allows the earpiece to spread farther out to fit more comfortably on your ears than a rigid piece.) The way we demonstrated that difference in the marketing materials was the same way ClearVision's sales people demonstrated it to their customers. They took the frame, held each end of the earpieces and pressed the frames virtually flat, 180 degrees, on a table without the frames or hinges breaking. Our ad used a picture of a hand on either end of the frames, holding it completely open so that the earpieces and eyepiece were both virtually flat. The headline was "Flexit. You can bend it, but you can't break it." The slogan was "Flat out, the best."

After we produced the ads for the trade, I saw the merchandising kit that Peter was sending out to retailers. It consisted of a sell sheet, display piece with cut outs for the actual frames, foam-backed counter mat for opticians to place in front of their customers, along with other display pieces. And then there were the other things they often produced, though all were not necessarily used for Flexit: a mailing piece, a feature in the company's newsletter, a trade ad, a display mat featuring the product or slogan, salesmen pieces, opticians' window displays, trade promotions and contests, and mini-brochures for consumers. Again, possibly the norm for the industry, but nothing was overlooked. Get the idea?

Good Idea:
- Your ad becomes a mailing piece
- Your ad is slipped into your brochure
- Your ad is sent to your trade publications

- Your ad is enlarged and put on your window, your waiting room, or your conference room
- Your ad is used as the basis of a PR release
- Your ad is put on your website
- Your ad is in your newsletter
- Your ad is sent to people you are certain will never care, because you will be pleasantly fooled more often than you think

Your ad is placed into your press kit. The one you have or will soon have overflowing with your brochure, mailings, fliers and every mention of your company.

13

TRUST YOUR TUMMY—
BUT DON'T FALL IN LOVE

It is never a good idea to break the rules until you actually know the rules. There will, however, be a moment when the time is right. It arises when you have been sticking very closely to your strategy, doing all the right things. Unexpectedly, but to your delight and amazement, a good idea literally pops up inside your head. You instantaneously know how to thoroughly develop the idea, how to utilize the whole carcass, how to obtain a little respectable PR from it. Except it is so far off the strategy you have developed that you are tempted to just toss it away. Except there is something about it; something smart and persuasive and distinctive and unexpected and, well, just so damn superior to your other ideas that immediately, instead of tossing it, you actually circle it, make it bold, and use a larger and different font so you can see it more clearly on your list to make certain you never lose it. That's an idea worth keeping and using and the heck with the rules. No one knows what you want to accomplish more than you do, and when it seems right, then it probably is.

William Goldman has written many books—*Boys and Girls Together* is a favorite of mine—and screenplays for movies such as *The Princess Bride* and *Butch Cassidy and The Sundance Kid.* One of his most quoted movie industry insights is "Nobody knows anything." Who am I—or anyone—to disagree and tell you to inflexibly always stick to your strategy?

Forget the logic, the rules, what others may say. Remember, your idea is delicate, like all ideas. Trust your gut feeling. *Non illegitimis carborundum.* (Not Latin, but close enough.) Of course, there are times when you will be wrong. The idea will really suck. But we'll discuss that later.

While you are still somewhat of a novice in the idea-generating business, you will probably fall in love with your work more often than after you have been doing it for a while. In the beginning, the excitement of seeing anything respectable on your blank page will be so rewarding you will fall in love too often and too easily, as you did when you were a teenager. When you gain experience and bring some perspective to your creations, you will add more objective judgment to what you consider good and what you consider not quite as good.

CASE HISTORY: VASELINE PETROLEUM JELLY

The creative assignment was appealingly wide open: develop a new television campaign for Vaseline Petroleum Jelly. The creative department was led into traditional directions by account executives who "knew" what the client was looking for. This was no time to do anything unexpected—not if you wanted to have a chance of having your work selected for the actual presentation to the client. I was called in, as was the entire team of creatives, to help out and generate ideas. All the ideas that were presented—some more clever to me than others—did exactly what they were supposed to. Each featured the very real benefits of Vaseline: removing make-up, protecting minor scrapes, being used as a moisturizer. But each commercial concept ignored what I considered the most important detail. That was, for lack of a better word, the "glop" factor of the product. Vaseline Petroleum Jelly is a viscous, thick, gelatinous product. Of course, no one in their right mind would ever talk about that, because, well, as an attribute, it is sort of unattractive, like that piece of spinach in your teeth. It may be there, it may be real, yet it is simply not pointed out. But I was drawn to it as an area that could yield unexpected results.

 Good Idea: Is there something about your Phufkel that is never mentioned, because you actually never noticed it or because you took it for granted? More important, is there a preconceived negative to your Phufkel that might actually be a benefit, depending on how it is presented to your target. Like the exceptionally strong bite of a mouthwash, which could be a negative but instead is presented as proof of its strength and efficacy. Maybe it is not a bad thing to look at your Phufkel again with fresh eyes and no preconceived notions. The difference could be small, like a counter sunk screw head that won't scratch the table, or something bigger like a GPS in your delivery van that allows you to track your deliveries in real time. Look at your Phufkel as if you had never seen it before, turn it over, take it apart. Look at it not with your own eyes, but those of your customers. If practical, show it to someone who has never seen it before to get a reaction. If you are lucky, you will get a response you didn't expect.

My commercial for Vaseline opened on a tight shot (close-up) of a beautiful woman. The camera pulls back to see her walking in a chrome/tile environment that suggests a swimming pool setting. As the woman walked toward us, she started to slide off her white terry bathrobe. The female announcer said, "Enjoy a refreshing dip before bedtime," as we cut to a close-up of the model's hand "dipping" into a jar of Vaseline petroleum jelly. The lady applies some to her shoulders, face, knee, and foot, while the announcer continues, "Let Vaseline Petroleum Jelly moisturize your body. Every place it touches it softens and soothes." We cut again to her hand dipping into the jar and then to her applying the product to her elbow. The announcer says, "Skin care experts know nothing moisturizes better, nothing softens better." We cut to the model applying Vaseline to her neck as the announcer says, "100% pure Vaseline Petroleum Jelly." Then a final cut to her hand dipping in. We freeze the frame as we superimpose the title, ENJOY A REFRESHING DIP, on the screen while the announcer finishes, "Enjoy a refreshing dip tonight."

The point, the good idea that my tummy said was something to be proud of, was the idea of equating a refreshing dip into a pool (or lake, pond, ocean, or fountain) and a dip into Vaseline. Because this was the only moisturizer that could make that claim and own that imagery, why ignore it when you could make it a unique benefit? The art director Jack Robertson and I presented the idea to the account executives. This was the meeting that would determine which ideas would make the cut. I actually believed that they would understand it, even embrace it. Instead, we were looked at as if we had presented a wine commercial that said the only reason to drink the stuff was to get tanked. Perhaps true enough, but no reason to ever mention it out loud. However, dipping was the good idea we believed in, and we told the account executives the reasons we believed in it and walked out.

No, there was no last-minute change of mind. There was simply no way that a commercial focused on the viscosity of the product would ever be shown to a client. The commercial died, existing today only as my dusty photocopy of the original storyboard. But the point of my book is to help you become skillful at creating good ideas, not just for me to brag about the successful ones.

Good Idea!

Good Idea: Let me point out a phrase in the Vaseline commercial: "Nothing moisturizes better, nothing softens better." This is what is called a "parity claim." It is a phrase that sounds preemptive and superior, but all it really is saying is that it is *as good as* others in the category. It is not saying it is better than the others, though the intention is certainly to imply superiority. You will have to decide when and if you want to use language like that. Some creatives consider it misleading, others use it when they feel that they have no other alternative for a claim. Personally, I feel very strongly both ways.

As you look for your good idea, you are bound to initially come up with advertising clichés. Think of those as the stretches you do before the real exercises start. Don't settle for that initial thought. Don't become fixated with the first thing—or anything—you create. Become attached. Be proud. Get serious. But don't ever marry an idea. Because if you find out, for a number of reasons, you can't use it, you won't be prepared to discover your new passion till you get rid of your attachment to your old love.

Good Idea!

Good Idea: Take a cliché, such as "the light at the end of the tunnel," and come up with different ways to verbalize that phrase. Keep in mind that the Phufkel in this case is a lighter/milder/less filling or lower caloried version of the original. This is a really tough undertaking. When the cliché truly fits it is often simply an impossible task to improve it. We certainly don't want to change it just for the sake of change. But it is worth attempting just to see if you can come up with something that is not as immediately familiar.

Here is another idea that I fell in love with. I presented the concept inside the ad agency, and it just never got anywhere. This was partially because I didn't want to make any changes that would make it safer and more similar to other advertising. I was so in love with the idea I resisted any changes, no matter how minor or how helpful they would have been in furthering the concept so that it might have been presented to the client. I was that much enamored. And that much pigheaded.

CASE HISTORY: ANACIN

The category was analgesics. The product was Anacin. This was an advertising exploratory, which meant let's see if we can come up with new campaigns to show the client.

I did what I have asked you to do: look at previous commercials for the Phufkel, look at competitive examples, develop ideas you think you can bank everything on, remember that the benefit you finally find has to be something the product can support, and perhaps most important, make certain you have not seen your good idea someplace else.

When, with little experience in that category, I looked at the compilation of various analgesic commercials, they did seem to be all rather similar. (From the point of view of an expert in the category, of course, I am sure there were many meaningful nuances.) The commercials were of people conducting on the street interviews, or testimonials, or often a mother complaining about her headache and then taking the product featured in the commercial. Lo and behold she is feeling better, no longer hollering at her children, and now baking a cake for her husband. Each spot usually included an abstract animated demonstration of why/how the product works. Basically the bulk of analgesic campaigns showed their own version of real-life situations, all treated very seriously.

There have been exceptions. I recall the Excedrin campaign, where they used numbers, such as Excedrin Headache Number 12, and each commercial had a warmly humorous feeling. Humor, though, is not what is typically used for a headache remedy. Which makes sense, since people with headaches are not known for their appreciation of the amusing side of their situation. (Though that did not stop me. Pigheaded, remember?)

My Eureka moment was when I realized that though we always saw people suffering from headache pain, we never saw the people or situations that were causing them the pain. We might first see screaming children, followed by the mother's pained reaction. But we usually quickly left the scene that showed the cause of the headache.

My good idea was that there are many daily situations that can give you a headache and it would be interesting to focus on the cause of the headache—the irritating, aggravating person or situation that was giving you the pain—rather than the cliché of focusing on the person who was in pain. In each of the commercials I created, the camera represented the viewer (this is called a subjective camera).

For example, in one commercial the viewer at home, watching the commercial, actually represented a passenger in the back seat of a taxi. The driver is turned around, facing the camera, and explaining to the passenger (television viewer) why they are in the midst of such a massive traffic jam. We hear exaggerated sound effects of traffic, horns, and chaos as we pick up the driver's voice during his explanation of the problem.

TAXI DRIVER: "Sure, I coulda taken the Triboro. But you figure that this time of the day, the tunnel right into Grand Central and then this little short cut. Did you know about the broken pipe? But it's not the last flight back today, right? Oh, well, there's a nice airport hotel . . ." At this point, while we still hear the driver, we cut to a bottle of Anacin and superimpose the title: What Would You Give For Some Anacin Right Now? (the driver has been continuing his prattle) ". . . if there's a bed. Hey, you like baseball? My cousin. . . ."

I must admit, after I wrote that spot I fell deeply and permanently in love with the concept. Think of it. We seemingly break all the rules and yet we really don't. We have a person in pain from a headache, but it is each and every viewer who is suffering, not the person on camera. And the theme line took advantage of the familiarity the viewer had of the product along with the implied superiority of Anacin (This kind of situation needs Anacin, not ordinary aspirin). Part of the charm of the spot to me was that it was only a 15-second commercial. This had media and budget implications for running the spots more often for less money or showing two different spots in one 30-second time period. The taxi driver spot could have been paired with another spot I created of a passenger seeing his cabin on a cruise ship for the first time. The cabin steward, the only one on camera, was busy explaining in a haughty and abrasive tone why this was indeed the cabin that had been requested. SHIP'S STEWARD: (talking straight into the camera, to the television viewer, as if it were the cruise passenger who had just complained to him about the room he was assigned) "No sir, what you requested was an inside double, not a stateroom. We cannot find a record of a stateroom in your name. And this is *not* a closet with cots. You can get an extra cot, though the room seems already as crowded as one might wish. And that engine rumble will assuredly be repaired mid-cruise, if the leak. . . ."

As in the other spots in the campaign, the person continues to talk thought the entire commercial. We cut away at the end, while still hearing him, to a shot of an Anacin bottle and the words on the screen: What Would You Give For Some Anacin Right Now?

Remember what else I suggested you do when you have your good idea? Figure out other ways to use it? (You know, the "use the whole carcass thing"?) Well, another reason I was so enamored with this campaign, falling deeper and deeper in love, was when I realized how it could be used in another entirely surprising but relevant manner. I realized that among other unexpected print possibilities, we could place a small ad in the real estate listings and another in the help wanted sections. Both sections are read by those who are feeling anxious and stressed. One group is looking for a new job and the other is contemplating the purchase of a new home. An ad with a picture of a bottle of Anacin in the middle of the section, with the eight-word message, "What Would You Give For Some Anacin Right Now?" was a perfect example to me of relevant shock.

The account team didn't quite see it the way I did. Depending upon the corporate culture of the ad agency, the assignment to develop startling new ideas for analgesics was code for "how about a longer demo in the middle, or maybe something as daring as an unusual colored title at the end." So this campaign also never made the final cut.

Now, if you are in charge of the marketing in your company, you will not face this problem. Being both the creative director as well as the decision maker ensures you will have better success in getting your ideas produced. But with that influence comes major accountability.

Sure, trust your tummy. But, just as in real life, be careful about falling head over heels.

14

WHAT'S IN A NAME?

When you started your search for your good idea, you looked at the strategy, the benefits of your Phufkel, what the competition had done, and what your company had already done internally. You wrote down phrases, words, themes, slogans, and headlines; in short, you did all the things you now know you are supposed to. There is an additional place to search for inspiration that might be so obvious you may not even spend time considering it. I am referring to the name of your Phufkel.

If your Phufkel has a distinctive name, it might be a good idea to try to tie it into your idea. Failing that, it might still be interesting enough as the basis of one ad or mailing piece.

Not every name will work, but if you consider it carefully, and put some effort toward creating a campaign or marketing piece around it, it can work to your advantage. It can, however, also lead you nowhere, or even worse, lead you to a dull idea. You don't want to force the fit, but for example. . .

Good Idea: Before I reveal examples of solutions I developed using product names as the basis of an idea, let me tell you the names. Then, without reading my solution, think of how you might use the name in a campaign, ad, slogan, or headline.

One brand was Tuck-It-Away, a self-storage company. But before reading the next section, think of some ideas and then come back when you are ready.

TUCK-IT-AWAY SELF-STORAGE

Tuck-It-Away is a company that has offered self-storage and mini storage in New York and New Jersey since 1980. Self-storage simply means that you rent, by the month, a storage space to which you have your own lock and key. You can rent anything from a small locker to a large room and use the space for just about anything: extra furniture, seasonal items, school stuff for the summer, virtually whatever you need the space for, short term or long. It's like an extra basement or attic for those who don't have one.

The creative challenge was to make Tuck-It-Away stand out from the competition. It had a smaller marketing budget and many fewer locations than its competitors, but nothing that couldn't be overcome with a good idea. I developed different approaches based on the usual claims and benefits in the category: convenience, low cost, use your own lock and key, and how much you could cram into a small space.

Here is an (abbreviated) collection of thoughts, random and purposeful, that I put down when I began my creative exploratory. Some ideas were for slogans, some for promotions, and some for ads. At this stage, as you know, you just write them down as you think of them, even creating your own strategies, editing the output later.

- ♦ Spaced Out?
- ♦ To show people how to fully utilize their storage space, hire a luggage packing authority (someone who has written an article in a travel guide on the most efficient way to pack a suitcase). Perhaps make that person the Tuck-It-Away spokesperson.
- ♦ Print and distribute turkey-stuffing techniques for Thanksgiving.
- ♦ Tuck-It-Away Introduces A New Space Program
- ♦ PR contest: how much can you stuff into a 4 × 6 Tuck-It-Away space?
- ♦ Hold Everything

♦ Do a promotion that offers to the renter, for a limited time, one size up at no additional cost (pay for a 4 × 4, get a 5 × 5).

♦ Maybe idea of we do only one thing (storage) other storage companies do two things (moving and storage).

♦ Ads for specials on things that most people have purchased and tucked away for years, like exercise bikes, Patti Page records, hula-hoops.

♦ Got stuff? Need space? Tuck-It-Away!

♦ A Room With No View

♦ Perhaps design an ad that looks like a real estate ad: Available small room, no view, free parking, free moving in, 00 square feet.

♦ We're less than 2 miles from most of you. The way you act, you'd think it was 200.

♦ Kangaroo for a symbol?

♦ Tuck-It-Away. We've got space for your stuff.

♦ Where are you going to put all those beanie babies when the next fad hits?

♦ You know that painting you bought at the street fair two years ago and then got tired of it and put it out on the street and that man found it and sold it to the Metropolitan Museum of Art last week for $12 million? Oh, heck, we said we weren't going to bring that up.

♦ Before you buy that new sofa, maybe you should figure out what to do with the old one.

♦ Merry Christmas. And what are you going to do with the gifts you got last Christmas?

Buried in that list was the genesis of the good idea, which, if you have read the title of this chapter, you already have figured out had something to do with the name. (I must admit, when we first got the account I thought the name was, if anything, a handicap.)

My insight was that another way of looking at why people needed storage space is that they wanted to store their possessions rather than discard them. Perhaps people thought their belongings would have more value in later years, maybe they wanted to save stuff for their kids, maybe they just couldn't bear to part with an object for sentimental reasons; whatever the reason this was my suggestion for them: Don't throw away all the stuff you really want to keep. Store it somewhere instead.

Said a different way, "Don't Throw It Away. Tuck-It-Away." It was a unique positioning, it talked to people who may not have realized that they had a choice of throwing stuff away or storing it, and most important, it was a good mnemonic for people to more easily remember my client's name and associate it with his business.

We presented, as usual, a group of ideas and stated which one was our favorite. I would like to say the client applauded when we made our recommendation. Instead, as a literate but literal man he asked, what about all the people who weren't thinking of throwing stuff away and just wanted to store it? My answer was that they would obviously understand what Tuck-It-Away offered, since it was indeed a self-storage company and they were familiar with that service. But here was a way to truly differentiate this company from all of the competing self-storage companies. All competitive slogans and signage dealt with the storage spaces they offered and how much stuff you could cram in them, rather than a claim and benefit Tuck-It-Away could own. Sure, we could still talk about storage and space, but that is a category given. We had a good differentiating platform to stand it all on. And he (eventually) agreed.

My favorite of the ads we produced was one with a headline that asked, "You know all the stuff you'd hate to throw away?" The solution then followed: "Now you don't have to." It ended with the slogan: Don't Throw It Away. Tuck-It-Away.

 Good Idea: When thinking about names, there may be a way for you to get a distinctive theme or even a name for your Phufkel by using a combination of the letters that make up your name. Sometimes you can make your name distinctive by something as simple as capitalizing a letter inside the name. Stardust as a name is different from StarDust and may help you stand out if, for example, your Phufkel is a home-cleaning product. Or perhaps try capitalizing the first and last letters of the name. (This is getting perilously close to creating a logo, but the intent is to have you look closely at the name of your Phufkel, to use it as part of a theme, or design it in such a way that it gains distinction.) Again, StardusT is different from Stardust or StarDust.

The famous Aflac quacking duck, as we all know, uses the quacking sound a duck makes to implant its name into the American conscious—and unconscious. Geico insurance used a gecko to attempt the same results, but in my opinion it was a strained approach to name recognition that never was as effective. First, you have to comprehend a "gecko" as a bad homonym for Geico. Then you have to ignore the fact that a gecko is a lizard, certainly not the cuddliest of icons. Finally, the commercials had the gecko use a British accent; perhaps it was to give it stature, perhaps to give it sincerity, perhaps, well, I just don't know.

CASE HISTORY: RAPID PARK GARAGES

Rapid Park, a group of approximately 30 garages in New York City, was a client of my agency for many years. One of the first assignments they gave us was to design a new T-shirt for them because one of their competitors had a T-shirt that stated they were the parking *professionals*. Rapid Park wanted one that said they were the parking *people*. (It could have been vice versa. But my point is the same.)

Remember, I have several handicaps when I begin to create ideas. One is that whenever possible I like to have a strategy to work with so that I know what problem I am attempting to solve. (You should also.) Two, I don't differentiate between creating an idea for a simple T-shirt or an idea for an elaborate national television campaign. Certainly there is a difference in importance in terms of media dollars, but I often devote the same amount of time seeking an idea for the little projects as I do for larger ones. However, as I have indicated, once you have a good idea, even for a T-shirt, you never know where it will lead.

We positioned Rapid Park as being just as qualified, experienced, and competent as the big boys. The strategy we developed in the agency was to convince building owners that they shouldn't automatically only send out proposals for bids to manage their building's garages to the usual suspects. There were indeed additional legitimate choices available, and they should add Rapid Park to their consideration set. (Yes, that's a lot to ask for a piece of cloth with four holes in it.)

I worked very hard and created about 20 different themes, tags, and headlines ideas for that T-shirt. When we had our meeting with the client, Kevin Wolf, president of Rapid Park, he must have thought that we were a little obsessive. He certainly knew that when you got right down to it it was only a T-shirt, and he had already said that all he wanted was something simple.

Good Idea: Overkill? Well, what if you were creating it for your own company? Wouldn't you consider it an important assignment? Or would you just say, "Gee, it's only a T-shirt. Who really cares?" Don't let me hear you think like that. Work diligently to create that good idea, be it for a T-shirt, window sign, brochure, 15-page insert in a magazine, international television campaign, whatever. Don't belittle the medium and use that as an excuse to do less than your best. Of course you have to prioritize your efforts to determine what might be reasonable expectations for your return on your time and efforts. But as I have promised you, a good idea takes on a life of its own and can build your business in ways you never thought of when you were struggling for something seemingly as trivial as a sign in your store window or on an easel at the trade show. So take the time, make the effort.

Originally, I didn't think there was much that could be done with the parking garage's name. If anything, I would have guessed that the "Rapid" part of the name would lead into more interesting directions than the simple "Park." But as I worked on the assignment one idea stood out, elbowing aside the others, and shouting, "Look at me, look at me." It was the idea we were recommending because we actually believed that the totally unexpected way it played off Rapid Park's name could make the client's brand stand out in a positive, unique manner. To Kevin's credit he bought the idea we suggested.

The visual had a straightforward, but intriguing look, art directed by John Twomey. On the front of the T-shirt was a black outline, representing Manhattan. Inside the outline, in the center, was a solid green rectangle, positioned so that it was clear that it was meant to represent Manhattan's Central Park. Scattered around the front of the shirt inside the outline of Manhattan were about a dozen green "R's," each one-inch high. They represented the various locations of Rapid Park garages. The theme that tied it all together, the "good idea" that positioned Rapid Park as a sensible, rational alternative for garage management contracts, was: "New York Has More Great Parks Than You Think."

This good idea, based on a name and originally developed for a T-shirt, brought the strategy to life and became the basis of a very successful marketing campaign lasting several years. It was used as the theme for Rapid Park's ads, mailing pieces, promotional material—basically everything that was created.

 Good Idea: Another time I ended up using a name as the basis for an idea was for a line of Freedom cameras from Minolta. Work with the name yourself and see what you might do with it, then see what I did.

MINOLTA FREEDOM CAMERAS

Differentiating this line of cameras from other cameras with similar features meant, to me, avoiding variations of "use my camera and your pictures will be better than with competitive cameras." My idea ended up featuring the

name of the camera, but this did not mean that I immediately realized that there was value in the name. At first, it
was just one on a long list of possible approaches.

My good idea was to feature cliché shots of classic
movie scenes where enslaved or imprisoned people have
no chance of ever gaining their freedom.

The storyboard for the commercial (used for the presentation, though never produced) opened on two exhausted,
emaciated galley slaves seated next to each other, pushing
the oars of a ship. They are gaunt, wearing tattered rags,
and having absolutely no chance of anything ever getting any better for them. One turns to the other and says,
"Don't worry, the captain has promised us our Freedom
tonight." The next scene is the classic movie dungeon
scene. Two other men had their wrists and ankles manacled to the rough cobblestone wall six feet above the
ground. Man One says, "I think I know how we can get
our Freedom." We next cut to the classic scene of a South
American country in revolution with an unruly, angry
crowd, arms raised, shouting up to their leaders on the
balcony, "Freedom. Freedom! Freedom!!" We then see
beauty shots of the actual cameras. To keep the freedom theme going, the announcer couched each distinct
claim in terms of guaranteeing the user various forms of
freedom: freedom from fumbling, with automatic film
loading; freedom from fear of out-of-focus pictures; and
freedom of choice, with one-touch wide angle or tele-
flexibility. We then cut back to the original dungeon
scene. With a camera in his still manacled hand, one of
the prisoners points it at his cellmate and says, "Smile."
When the flash goes off the screen goes white and leads
us to a shot of the cameras and Minolta's tag line.

That's what I did with the name "Freedom." What did
you do?

15

PECKED TO DEATH
BY DUCKS

There you are with your good idea—an ad, a brochure, a commercial, whatever. Maybe, though, you feel you should get someone else's opinion. You want to bounce it off someone—at most just a few people—who have not seen it before or been part of the creative process. You are having doubts, questions, misgivings, and qualms that it is not understandable enough, good enough, or even strategically the correct message.

While getting some objective opinions is not bad, be careful. The first problem is what is sometimes called "secretary research," whether it involves a real secretary or not. You ask a secretary in the office or someone in the mailroom or even a delivery person to look at your idea because you feel you will get a nonpolitical, honest opinion.

You won't.

In the famous first place, as soon as you ask people for their opinion, they are put in the position of having to offer an opinion, whether they want to or not or have one or not. They suddenly behave as if they are experts on the subject (Why else would you solicit their input?) and often give answers they think will make them look knowledgeable, no matter what they are really thinking. This is true even if you ask the question in a completely unbiased manner, which is never easy. Then again, they may not want to hurt your feelings, or, alternatively, may relish that prospect.

Good Idea: There is a test you can apply to see if the person you are asking to look at your idea will provide an insight that is worth listening to. If you ask the person what the "idea" is and the response has nothing to do with the idea, then you should say thanks and go on to the next person on your list. For example, suppose you are looking for feedback on a toothpaste ad. You ask what they think the main message is that the ad is trying to communicate. If the response is, "That reminds me, I have to go the dentist," or "I never use that brand," you are not really getting the help you wanted. It is not easy for people to judge an idea or even to always recognize one. (Like you perhaps, before you read this far.)

Another reason to treat your secretary research with some caution is the basic fragility of an idea. A good idea is like a balloon; while it can soar high above the commonplace, all it takes is one little prick to destroy it forever.

If you ask enough people their opinion of a headline, for example, and each person only changes one word, you soon will not recognize your original thought. Being pecked to death by ducks simply means that while you do not feel any individual bite, you end up dead just the same. It is similar to the death by 1,000 cuts you hear so much about; it somehow seems less threatening, though it is just as deadly.

CASE HISTORY: DRAMBUIE LIQUEUR

It was a new business pitch for Drambuie, an after dinner drink that is a blend of scotch whiskies, heather honey, and, naturally, a secret ingredient. There was lots of pressure, and lots of prestige for the winning creative, and therefore lots of politics involved within the agency. The odds of anyone other than a very senior creative (which I was not) having their work considered was, well, you know the usual story. First, though, a question: How many people do you know who drink Drambuie? Let me broaden that question. How many people do you know who have even heard of Drambuie? Which led me into the direction of scarcity equaling prestige; that is, only a special few can recognize its special qualities. While I was tempted to go down that road, I didn't want to go over the usual well-traveled testimonial path. I wanted to focus on the fact that Drambuie was rarely served before or during a meal. It was only served following a meal. In spite of realizing I had no chance—or maybe because that realization freed me to try anything I wanted— I found myself with the idea of using arresting black and white portraits of famous influential historic icons. Each of them was a significant leader in whatever field they were involved with. The good idea was not just the unusual look of the page. It was the combination of words that was the headline in every ad in the campaign.

For example, you had photos of three impressive notables in one ad: Andy Warhol, Winston Churchill, and George Bernard Shaw. Then there was a headline writ large: "There Have Been Many Great Leaders . . . But Only One Great Follower."

Next to the bottle, at the bottom of the ad, was this claim: "Drambuie Liqueur. Nothing Follows A Great Dinner Better."

It was dignified, associated the product with famous and exalted people, and was an admirable play on leaders and followers. Larry Paolucci, the art director, brought the idea to life with a look, tone, and feel that was exceptional, as was usually the case with Larry. The page was entirely black and white; the only color was the bottle of Drambuie. Because it was a good idea, more potential versions than I could keep track of kept leaping onto the page. Another mockup used black and white photos of Hemingway, Picasso, and General Eisenhower. One version used 16 different photos of leaders from all different fields—politics, science, theater, and sports—along with the same campaign headline and theme.

I even thought the concept through to the point where I did not want to indicate anywhere in the ad exactly who the people portrayed actually were. I felt it would be more intriguing and get more involvement if people looked at the ad, identified those faces that they could, and asked their friends for the other names.

There were also the ads targeted to specific audiences: golf celebrities for golf magazines, theater celebrities for entertainment sections, sports stars for magazines like *Sports Illustrated,* business leaders for *Fortune* and *Forbes,* and so on.

Agreed, it was a good idea. Even top management of the agency in charge of the presentation recognized its worth and praised it. And then came what you have to beware of: being pecked to death by ducks.

The first thing that happened to my good idea was the suggestion from a high-ranking creative that perhaps it should not be famous leaders and followers. It should be famous endings, like the demolition of Ebbets Field. So that had to be worked up for him. Then another biggie creative suggested making the leaders less formidable and more approachable so the common folk could relate to them. And be sure to include the names of each celebrity, so that the reader would never feel ignorant. Another suggestion was to just put one person in each ad. I don't remember all the suggestions, but the net effect was to dilute the idea beyond saving. Yet, I must admit I listened to them all. Partly because they had never been so involved with any of my previous work at the agency.

Partially because part of me said, well they are the top hierarchy of the shop, so they must be better than their comments make me feel they are.

Then came the next internal presentation. The president of the agency, who had seen only my initial idea and not the various changes, took one look and got very upset. With me! He dismissed the idea and said in effect that I had no idea how good the original campaign was and that I had destroyed it with what I was showing him now. I looked around for support from those in the meeting who had led me down this path. (I am still waiting.)

The end result was that the campaign was not shown. (By the way, the agency did not get the account. The campaign recommendation, as I recall, was a photo of a man entering his home after a difficult day and saying to his wife, "Do Me A Drambuie." No comment.)

Good
Idea!

Good Idea: How you can resolve the inevitable differences of opinion as you bounce your ideas off others? While there is nothing inherently wrong with getting other people's views, how do you decide who has the final word? My partner and I developed a solution early on. We always show whatever we have created—ad, media plan, strategic direction—to each other for a fresh viewpoint. But whoever signs the document gets the final say. I don't literally mean, "sign," as in a signature on the bottom of a letter or e-mail. I mean whoever has created the piece and is responsible for it decides how much of the other person's input he will use. You may want to keep this principle in mind. Listen closely and welcome the inevitably different points of view. Then it is your responsibility and obligation to do what you still feel is the right thing.

Be careful also of being too polite. To keep the animal analogies coming, "A camel is a horse designed by a committee" applies here. This is different from changing a word or two to accommodate someone. It happens when you add a few thoughts to your original piece to placate the person who made the suggestion. Perhaps you owe them one or want to make them feel part of the solution. Be aware that most of the time it weakens the idea.

Resistance to being pecked to death does not mean being inflexible and never making changes. Sometimes you will want to; sometimes you will feel forced to. The following example demonstrates the latter: Wheat Stax was a cereal from General Mills that was going into a test market. It had a roughly circular shape, about the size of a quarter, was almost a quarter of an inch thick, and had a honeycomb shaped interior. It was remarkably crunchy because it was not flat like an ordinary flake. Its interior ridges and hollows provided many toasted interior surfaces that gave additional crunch. My idea was that they were toasted on the front, back, inside, and outside. My slogan was "New Wheat Stax. Toasted In Places Other Cereals Don't Even Have Places."

That's what I presented to my boss, who promptly put in his two cents, or in this case, his one word. He insisted on changing the line from "Toasted In Places Other Cereals Don't Even Have Places" to "Toasted In Places Where Other Cereals Don't Even Have Places." Read it again if you didn't at first see what he did; he added the word "where" to the already lengthy line. I argued for about three minutes and then folded, realizing that the campaign would never get out of his office without accepting that change. Looking back, I realize that it was not such a terrible trade-off. I gave in to adding one completely unnecessary word in exchange for giving my boss a sense of ownership in the phrase, so he would fight to see that it was produced, which it was.

Being pecked by ducks can lead to a gruesome ending, or at best a quick painless death. You have to be strong enough to resist the most well-meaning of intentions because whether it is quick bites or slow nibbles, your idea will end up with no discernible pulse.

LITTLE THINGS CAN MEAN A LOT

A good idea doesn't have to be a big deal. Oh, it becomes big because it stands out and gets attention. But it shouldn't scream, "Hey, look how exceedingly clever I am," especially if the cleverness overwhelms the message you are trying to get across.

Sometimes it is the smallest of things that helps your theme or claim become more noticeable, provocative, and clever. Occasionally, it is a little thing itself that makes an idea good. But often it is the little things you do to your communication that add up, complement the idea, and actually help make it good.

You'll discover there are many areas where you can improve the feel and look of your message. Objects on the page are examples of some of these little things: the copy breaks, the placement of the illustration, the punctuation, the typeface, and the white space.

Have you looked over your typefaces? Have you used too many simply because you can? What about the size of your fonts? How many variations do you have? Is the art positioned exactly where you think it should be? Is the overall tone and voice of the communication appropriate for the Phufkel you are marketing? Are headlines broken at the logical best place or have you left a bad copy break such as an "and" sitting at the end of a line, forcing the next line to start off without any support at all. Which one, for example, do you think reads more easily?

NOW IS THE TIME FOR ALL GOOD MEN TO COME TO
THE AID OF THEIR COUNTRY
(or)
NOW IS THE TIME FOR ALL GOOD
MEN TO COME TO THE AID OF THEIR COUNTRY

(or)

NOW IS THE TIME FOR ALL GOOD MEN

TO COME TO THE AID OF THEIR COUNTRY

(If you did not select the last one, we are both in big trouble.)

Spell checking and correct grammar are little things also, but you better be sensitive to them both. Spell check everything. And then check it again. Typos will kill you. "Complimentary" and "complementary" will not always be caught by spell check, but they will certainly be caught by many of your readers. As will, "they're," "there," and "their" if used incorrectly. (I recently received a mailing that used the headline "It's not what their saying . . . It's what you're hearing." Well, at least they got the "you're" right.) Use the web to help you with grammar or buy a book such as *The Mac Is Not A Typewriter* by Robin Williams.

Here are some "little" examples of what I mean:

- ◆ A napkin from a Subway store. It has a listing of grams of fat and indicates what happens when you add 1 tsp. of olive oil to your sandwich. Except that they call it Oijve oil.
- ◆ The label from a package of Entenmann's Honey Blueberry Muffins. It said *"Net Wt. 16 Oz. (1 LB.). Unit Price per LB: 2.69. You pay $2.79."* I kept it for a while, intending to send it to them and ask why they wanted to charge me that additional 10 cents (hoping they would send me some sweet reward), but I finally did what most of us would do, I lost it.

These are easy to forgive and understand, but not something you want to do if it can be avoided—and it can be.

Here are some examples of *good* little things that have made an impression on me. Though they were not big enough to truly be considered good ideas of and by themselves, they were clever, distinctive, and good examples of what kinds of little things make a difference. If you don't have a good idea, the communication will suffer. However, if you overlook the opportunity these kinds of little things can offer, the idea will still be a good one, but you will have overlooked an opportunity to make your communication be all it could be.

Like many advertising copywriters, I spent time as a freelancer. My business card had all the normal, necessary information: name, address, phone, fax, website, and e-mail address. Then I added one thing more, not an icon, not a slogan, not a logo. Across the bottom of the card, in a small serif font, I added the entire alphabet: abcdefghijklmnopqrstuvwxyz. It was unexpected, curiosity provoking, and somehow seemed right. When asked what those letters were doing there, I answered, truthfully, "Those are the tools, the only tools that I have to work with. So I thought I'd feature them." A little thing, but one that helped me stand out from other freelancers in a subtle, imaginative manner without relying on an overproduced, four-color card, or a desperate attempt at cleverness.

Good Idea: As you can appreciate, I have been handed quite a number of business cards over the years. They have ranged from odd sized, two-sided, round, and multicolored to the common black and white. Some cards were filled with information, some sparse. Some used more fonts than I have on my computer. Some left you wondering what business the person who handed you the card was in.

So please, take out your card and hand it to your-self. What does it say about you? Does it reflect your company's personality? Is it too clever? Too sophisticated? Can you read your name, title, company, and address without squinting? Is whatever you consider the most important part of the information on the card the most prominent? All these are little things, but we now know how important they can be. Act accordingly.

Speaking of business cards, I did one for Bonita Porte's Energetic Juniors. Based in Manhattan, it offers in-home personal fitness training for children and teens. After several false starts, (Sure, blame the agency.), Bonita finally got her website up and running. While we obviously wanted to get the word out about her new site with a mailing and publicity, we also came up with a nice "little" thing. We printed new business cards, putting the new website address in red. Nothing else was in red, just the website. Now, the temptation for the client of course was, as long as we were spending the money for a second color, why restrict it to just the web address? How about the company name, too? And certainly the slogan merited extra attention, didn't it? Especially since the price for more ink was already covered.

But the whole point in only putting the web address in the second color was to draw attention to it. Add more lines of color and nothing would stand out. Taken to an extreme, putting everything in red would have been the same as leaving everything in black. The red was for emphasis, and that's why it was only used for one thing. A little thing, perhaps, but a good example of how a little thing can make a difference.

Good Idea: Think of what you've created for the marketing of your Phufkel that could benefit from a little tweak, a slight change, an unexpected use of color, type face, phrasing, or punctuation. When you have a piece that you are happy with and are getting set to produce, you should try to make the time to re-examine it. Without driving yourself crazy by second-guessing yourself into a stupor of inaction, experiment with the layout, the copy, and the graphic. (Of course, do all this only after you have saved the original version. Make your changes only on the "saved as" versions. Or you will hate yourself. And not be too happy with me, either.) Please, resist the temptation to turn a little thing into a big thing; use your tweaks sparingly. While one or two spoons of sugar can make your coffee more palatable, the fifth and sixth spoonfuls will ruin the taste.

Here's another Energetic Juniors example that illustrates how little things can be used to get big results. One of the tasks Bonita had her independent contractors do every month was send her write-ups of each class they taught, so that there would be a record of what the child's goals were, what specifically was being accomplished, how well the child was doing, what the child enjoyed or disliked, and which were the areas that could be improved. Read an abbreviated version of one of the reports and see if you can spot the opportunity.

OVERVIEW OF WORKOUT/GOALS

NAME is a delightful 13-year-old girl. She is very willing to work and even asks for exercises during the week. She is very serious about improving her posture and works hard. After discussion, we determined her goals to be:

1) Posture—particularly to remedy shoulders rounded forward and a pronounced "sway-back," an over-arching of the lower back
2) Stamina—ability to continue to play sports/go to the gym/swim or do any aerobic activity and not be winded or overly fatigued
3) Coordination—linking movement together grace-fully and safely
4) Flexibility—especially needed due to very tight hamstrings, hip joints (this in turn causes some of her back issues due to compensation by the spine)

Workout:

Warm up: 10 – 12 Minutes
Slow warm up of all muscles and tendons, stretches, toning, body alignment. Loosening hip, knee, and shoulder joints for larger range of motion. Posture, placement, and balance exercises.

Upper body pulses and Resistance Bands: 10 Minutes
This sculpts arms, adds strength, burns calories, and accelerates metabolism.

Mat Work: 20 Minutes
Abdominal strength and core placement: crunches, leg extensions, and spinal twists, "plank," "sphinx," and yoga stretches.

Dance/cardio/stamina: 15 Minutes
This is our more fun movement section – jumps, hopscotch, waltzes, dance combos, and coordination exercises.

Cool Down: 5 Minutes
Standing, balance checks and holds. Deep lunges, very slowly so heart rate returns to normal.

Comments
NAME is a hard worker at our sessions and very agreeable. To achieve her posture goals she does need to strengthen her abs, lengthen her hamstrings, and in general engage in enough movement/sports to develop her coordination further. This will also help her maintain her excellent health and body weight.

This is a fine, thorough and informative report. There is no problem with the content, but there was a lost opportunity for Energetic Juniors. Years ago parents weren't aware of these reports and were never given a copy of them! Though it was important for Bonita to have the reports, she did not at first realize how much value there could be in providing a copy to the parent. It was a little thing that would be easy enough to do, either by e-mail or enclosed with each month's invoice. This would help them to understand the depth of the service they were receiving, that it was not merely the hour the trainer spent with their child that they were paying for. They would recognize that there was much effort involved behind the scenes, before and after each session, which was not restricted to only the scheduling of sessions or providing the appropriate trainer for their child. Importantly, in the spirit of using the whole carcass, the reports were already prepared. All that had to be done to get the additional benefit from them was to get them to the parent.

 Good Idea: Don't be so good at keeping secrets. What do you have that you should be sharing with your customers and prospects? I don't mean all the good new ideas you now have that you will be getting the maximum use out of by using the whole carcass. I mean the stuff you have that has been lying around collecting dust instead of attention. What about an engineer's report that points out how your Phufkel exceeds industry standards? Or perhaps you have a letter of praise from a client that so far has been seen only by your secretary and yourself? Spread the word, and send a copy. It is another little thing, but an easy way—you don't have to create anything, just duplicate it—to get your Phufkel in front of people.

Another little thing I liked was a billboard for British Airways. They were introducing a better bed in First Class, and the ad was a simple picture showing the spaciousness of the bed, looking big, inviting, and oh so comfortable. The ad had a one-word headline. Well, not quite even an entire word. What they did was remove the "in" from the word "insomnia" and use the letters that were left as the headline: Somnia. It was a really good idea, one that got the reader involved because it was unexpected and the person quickly made the connection that if insomnia meant you weren't able to sleep well then naturally the word somnia that was coined obviously meant that you were able to sleep. A little, little thing it was, just removing two letters, but what a wonderful way to make the billboard into a good idea.

Here's one more example to illustrate the point that there is a wide range of little things you can do to promote your business. At a previous agency we were pitching a footwear company. My suggestion was that the three of us who were going to the new business meeting should each wear a pair of the shoes that our prospective client manufactured. So we went to a shoe store, bought three pairs of his shoes, and wore them to the meeting. We didn't say a word about them and neither did they. After we got the account, I asked if they had noticed; the answer, with a smile, was "yes." Were the shoes the reason we got the account? Nope. But it was a little thing that was favorably noted.

Okay, here's one more. At the Porte de Vanves flea market in Paris I purchased something because I thought it was a brilliant marketing idea. Of course, since I only speak sufficient French to make certain I will never be lost or hungry, I would not swear that this is what the vendor actually explained to me about my purchase. But it is a story I have repeated often enough to believe it. The object I purchased was a two-piece glass set. One piece was a flat, clear glass plate, salad plate size, with decorative glass bumps along the outer edge. The second part was a clear glass container, decoratively crosshatched, shaped and sized like an ice cream cone. The glass cone was sitting on the plate when I picked it up, asking what it was used for. As it was explained to me, the set was used in vineyard wine stores for customers to sample the wines prior to their purchase. The aspect that made it a good marketing idea was that after the owner had poured a taste of wine for you and you had finished with your glass, there was no obvious or simple way to put the glass down. You couldn't put it down on its narrow end, as it couldn't be balanced that way. Somehow it seemed impolite to turn it upside down and put it back down on the glass plate as if you were rejecting the wine and signaling a negative "thumbs down." So what could you do with the empty glass? If it worked as intended, you would just stand there and they would pour some more wine into your glass, which they were prepared to do as often as necessary till your sales resistance evaporated.

A (LITTLE) CASE HISTORY: HOST APPAREL

Host Apparel was a large manufacturer of private label loungewear, robes, and pajamas. We produced a series of ads, public relation pieces, articles, and mailings for them along with other marketing material. The point here, however, is of a little thing that I did when we were preparing material for a trade show in Las Vegas—MAGIC, a big fashion and apparel event that takes place twice a year. We were sending a mailing announcing all the latest products that would be at the Host booth: new fabrications and finishes, new solid and yarn-dyed twills, new gift-giving packaging, and other newsworthy items. So far, so expected. Then I realized that most of the participants and potential Host customers would be flying to the trade show, which led me to think of something that might actually be used before the show, on the flight. The good idea was to create a Host Apparel Word Find, a game that was popular before the Sudoku craze and is still played today. It consists of a grid of seemingly random letters, with a list of words underneath. The listed words are all in the grid, written either forward, backward, or on an angle. The object was to find all the words on the list, circling each one as you found it. My list consisted of words that were associated with Host Apparel, its brands, and new features, such as Bill Blass, sand wash, combed cotton, twill, and Diplomat. The instructions were to bring the correctly filled out puzzle to Host's booth to receive the special prize.

It was a good idea because the cost was a piece of paper, not even additional postage since we were sending out new product information in the same envelope anyway (use the whole carcass). Creating the Word Find was easy; I found a piece of freeware on the web (free). It gave the customer something different and fun to actually do on the plane (involving). It had the client's booth number on the page and an incentive to fill it out and bring it to the Host booth (relevant). It was indeed a good idea, though, in essence, it was just a little one. As you now realize, small good ideas can work wonders.

17

WHEN IS A GOOD IDEA
NOT A GOOD IDEA?

Everyone knows the joke about the secret of the proper timing of a punch line for a comedian. For the two of you who may not, here is how it goes: Person One says, "Ask me what the secret of telling a good joke is." Person Two replies, "What is the sec . . ." Person One interrupts, "Timing!"

Improper timing is one reason why a good idea suddenly can become a not-so-good idea. Here is an example of an idea I had a while ago that I thought would make a good idea if we ever pitched an airline. The campaign was designed for business travelers, not leisure market vacation tourists. Since it was never actually produced, I had the advantage of an unlimited budget. The commercial could be as many minutes long as my imagination required it to be. Visually, we see a business traveler in a comfortable business class environment. The cabin is half empty, and our hero has a comfy aisle seat. He is offered food and beverages by an exceedingly attentive and glamorous stewardess whose only job, it seems, was taking care of our passenger. He ate, drank, reclined, watched a movie, and in brief, had a truly wonderful experience. We then see him after landing, with quick cuts of the hassle of getting his luggage, then finding a taxi, the dense traffic on the way to the hotel, the lost room reservation, and the many employees with hands out for gratuities. When he finally enters his room we notice the accommodations are not particularly inviting: A small space, no view, non-working lamps, and one skimpy towel in the bathroom. In this prototypical introductory spot there was no announcer till the end, just appropriate music: heavenly during the flight, discordant once he lands. Our hero plops discontentedly down in the only chair in his room, a worn seat that barely fits his frame. We cut back to the scenes of him as he was on the plane, with great food, ample drink, and attentive stewardess, as the announcer states what by now is clearly obvious, "We may just be the best part of your trip."

The idea was generic, meaning any airline could have used it. But it also would have been preemptive, meaning the first one to use the idea ought to have been able to own it.

The problem is that the time has passed when this might have been a good idea. The hassle of airline travel is as bad now as the hotel scenes in that spot. Today there are the long lines, security searches, and ever-changing lists of what is acceptable to carry on board. When you do finally board, often there is little or no food offered, no pillows or blankets, crowded seating, long take-off delays, and other tribulations. So for now, and the fore-seeable future, it is unlikely that any airline travel will prove to be the best part of anyone's trip.

> Good Idea: When you come up with your good ideas, do not dilly and do not dally. Aside from the fact that circumstances may suddenly change rendering your good idea unusable, often ideas take form in the collective unconscious. People are exposed to the same facts, the same entertainment vehicles, and the same news programs. Given similar stimuli, the same basic thought—the premise of the good idea—could arise in more than one person. Get there first.

Aside from timing, what else can change a good idea into a bad idea? Many things. For another example, at one time the Stage Deli was interested in promotional items that they could hand out to customers. I came up with a good idea that was strategic, and yet completely unexpected. Not such a good idea, however, because . . . well, you'll see. Remember, a strategy of the Stage Deli was to convince its customers that even though its prices were New York skyscraper high, so were the size of the portions and quality of the food. My promotional product idea was a plastic ruler, eight inches in length. But instead of showing the numeral "five" at the five-inch mark, it would say "pastrami sandwich." At the six-inch point, instead of showing "six," it would indicate "cheese-cake." At the eight-inch mark, "triple decker." It was a graphic way of showing how enormously high the sand-wiches and cakes were and how much value you received for your dollar.

Yes, a good idea. But what would have been a better idea was to first get a budget from the client and obtain some estimates for the manufacturing of the rulers. What we discovered was that to produce them was sim-ply too expensive to hand out to customers, even if we could have gotten some valuable PR from the idea. Thus another time a good idea is not a good idea is when you discover after the fact that the budget won't accommo-date the thought.

Then there is the often good idea of having special promotions or reduced-price sales to sell more Phufkels during your ordinarily slower times. I don't necessar-ily mean the holiday sales events, presidential birthday promotions, or heaven forbid, the going-out-of-business sales, but rather the annual or infrequent sales that make the event—and the promised savings—seem legitimate. But the way to quickly ruin this good idea is with the theory, well, if one sales event a year is good, think how successful 12 would be.

There is a small chain of men's apparel stores where it is difficult to find a time of the year when they are not having a special sales event, each theoretically for a limited time: "Buy one get one free," followed soon after by "All suits just $179," replaced by "Four days only sales event," then "50 percent off everything." When you are constantly having sales, customers assume that the normal daily pricing is way out of line and that only during the many sales periods are the items in fact being sold for their true value.

Related to this is the good/bad idea of, well, if a magician were to do it, I guess you would call it misdirection. You take an intriguing premise and promise, but when it comes to the payoff the benefit is so scrawny compared to what the headline promised that it just is not a good idea. A headline that asks the intriguing question, "What would you do with up to six extra hours every week?" is a good enough idea. Then, as you read the copy, you realize that what is being offered is a service that will reorganize your office so that there is less clutter and mess, therefore saving time and effort in getting things done. Six hours? Every week? I don't think so.

Good Idea: Whenever you can, it is a good idea to avoid "weasel" words, the words in the copy that take away from what the headline promised. In the above example, it is the "up to." "Up to six extra hours" could literally mean as few as 10 minutes. This is not the kind of clever idea you should use to promote your Phufkel. If you think you should ask a lawyer to tell you if your copy is legal, it probably isn't a good idea to use it, no matter what the answer is. If you want to build a long-term business, take the higher ground.

CASE HISTORY: YOUR PHUFKEL

This case history is not from any specific case history of mine. It is from one of yours. I trust that as you have been using this book you have been developing ideas. Or perhaps you have been refining ideas you have thought of in the past. No doubt there have been several times when you have developed an idea that had absolutely no relationship with your creative strategy. But you became enamored of the thought, falling deeply in love with the idea. I even know your exact words. You recognized your dilemma, weighing the beauty of the idea with the reality that it really wasn't based on what you knew was the proper underpinning. But you just couldn't bring yourself to toss it into the reject pile. So you said, "Oh, just this once."

Not a good idea. Oh, I know I have told you to trust your tummy if you think the idea is worth it. But the decision comes down to this: How many times have you said, "Just this once"?

Also, while it is indeed a good idea to refresh a campaign, it is not a good idea to scuttle it too quickly. You may have the ability to create ideas very rapidly. That is often good; what can be bad is changing your ideas to a newer one every three seconds without giving the current ideas a chance to do their job. You may tend to love your latest child (idea) the most and can't wait to see it in action. Or you suffer from what is called corporate boredom. I have seen it in action and it can destroy many good ideas. What it means is that, for example, in an ad agency, you have presented your storyboards to the client. Then you present it to the top-level decision maker. You make all the changes requested and go back to the same people, who usually have just one more little tweak they want to make. So you make the little changes and go back to the client. Then you take it to the top person again, who looks at it basically for the third time and says something like, "I have seen this idea before, don't you have anything new to show me?" Remember, no consumer has seen it at all. It is just your client who has pecked it to death and is now tired of it.

If you quickly get tired of your ideas, changing them in favor of your newest ones, your customers will never have a chance to figure out who you are. Stuart Elliott, advertising columnist in the *New York Times*, puts it this way: "As the attention spans of consumers seem to shorten daily, and the conditions of the consumer marketplace seem to shift continuously, campaigns probably need to be freshened faster than they were in the past."

Notice he says "freshened faster,"*not* replaced more often.

The final two examples of when a good idea is not a good idea come from the new business archives of Porte Advertising. In hindsight, it is easy to see why some of the ideas did not work. At the time, however, I was bewildered.

The Blind Date

Early in Porte's history, I came up with a good idea for getting new business. In the copy of an early version of our agency brochure was something about understanding why prospective clients might not want to commit themselves to a long-term relationship with us. So we would be willing to take on a project to demonstrate how good we were. The way I wrote it compared it to going on a blind date; maybe it would work out and lead to a long association, or maybe it would be over after the initial meeting, with little harm done to either party. This pleasant enough metaphor led to an interesting thought, and I decided to bring the idea to life. Instead of sending out a bunch of new business solicitation letters, we selected the prospects we thought were most promising and sent the top choice a bouquet of flowers. Attached was a note that said only that we were interested in having a blind date. No company name, no signature, no return address, and no other words. Our hope was that the receptionist/gatekeeper would remember the flowers when we called and get us through to her boss. With a little luck, she might be the one to end up with our bouquet on her desk.

It worked! I called, said we were the ones who had sent the flowers, asked for a meeting, and bingo! One letter, one new business meeting.

And bingo! One new business meeting, no new business.

Now, you don't expect to convert every new business meeting into something concrete. Even with a good marketing idea to get you into the meeting in the first place, it usually takes a lot more wooing than one meeting as you get to know each other. But we never got the second meeting with the prospect. We tried the blind date gambit one more time, with the next company on our list. We had the same results: one meeting, no further interest.

Looking back, I think I know why. Our good idea was so much better than what we had to say about ourselves, it worked to our disadvantage. We had set up expectations about Porte—clever, outlandish, creative, determined— that we couldn't fulfill. We hadn't yet learned how to properly present ourselves or how to position ourselves. Also, we did not have a meaningful range of work for existing clients that we could show to demonstrate how good we were. The blind date idea was a good idea. It just came about too early in our business life.

Good Idea: As you would with your computer, make sure you have backup for your idea. This does not mean that you have a new/better idea finalized and ready to go, though that is not a bad plan. What I mean is that if it is a marketing idea to introduce your new Phufkel, make sure you have more than enough inventory available to fill the demand beyond your wildest expectations. Because if not, then your next good idea will have to be to figure out how to phrase the e-mail saying to your customers that they will have to wait till heck freezes over before you can get your new Phufkel to them. Also, everyone in your company should know about and understand the new Phufkel and your marketing plans. If it's a new ad campaign, set up a screening for your employees. Give everyone T-shirts with the new logo and slogan. Yes, everyone, because all employees should be able to discuss what is new in your company. In your heart you know that when the phone calls come in from the media wanting more information, the last person you think will get the call will be the first person to answer the phone.

The Grocery Bag

One of the things we had done when we started our agency was to make a list of all the separate products and categories we had worked on in our previous large-agency lives. We talked about how this big-agency, major-brand experience would be impressive to the smaller clients we were seeking.

Then I had a good idea. Just as the flowers brought the idea of a blind date to life, there was a way we could bring our large-brand experience to life. We might impress possible prospects with the household names that we had separately created marketing for by showing them the actual products. So I got a large paper grocery bag, and we put in a Sharp watch, small toy refrigerator, a single-serve box of Trix cereal, a small bottle of Ivory liquid, a miniature Campari bottle, a jar of Anacin, a Quaker granola bar, a 3 Musketeers bar, a Hamm's Beer bar tap, a stuffed animal Fruit Stripe Zebra, a pack of Beechnut gum, a toy phone, and a Snickers bar.

For our next new business meetings we took along the grocery bag, filled with our props. After we introduced ourselves I started emptying the bag, displaying the items that I was convinced would dazzle them with the breadth of experience we had on major brands. It was also an unusual, fun, creative icebreaker.

It just didn't work. Maybe because it was too cute. Perhaps prospects didn't really make the connection between a $30 million brand and their own smaller business. Maybe we gave up on it too soon because it was a very heavy bag to drag around town. But a good idea is not a good idea when it simply doesn't work.

Good Idea: Don't give up on an idea as quickly as we did. We were young and I was impatient. Also, I knew I could come up with other good ideas. But I should have given the blind date and the grocery bag ideas another chance and given some more thought to figuring out what the real problem was. If you really believe in your good ideas, take the time to think about how to make them successful.

18

DON'T BE SHY

Never assume that what you have to say is of no importance and little interest. Go ahead and mail, fax, or e-mail that press release. Write that ad or direct mail piece. Publish that blog. Put up that banner. It is like the punch line where the man says, "Why am I telling you? I'm telling everyone!"

Believe it to be newsworthy and others will begin to share your enthusiasm. The importance of your news is often judged by how importantly you treat it. If it is worth the time and effort for you to do it up right, the recipient is more likely to be impressed than if you merely "mumble" the information. Dress your occasion up with a fresh, good idea and it is more than likely that what you are promoting will be taken more seriously. If you want the world to marvel at your news, make your story as marvelous as possible.

What if you do not have big, earthshaking news? Put a fresh coat of paint on the news you do have. Give it a twist, turn it inside out, put a positive spin on it, and come up with a good idea to tell the world news such as:

- It's your business's birthday
- Your company has relocated
- You joined an organization
- You were made an officer of an organization
- You/your company received an award
- You received a thank-you letter from a customer
- You have produced a new Phufkel
- You have created an improved Phufkel
- Someone famous bought a Phufkel from you
- You contributed a Phufkel to an auction
- You've had a staffing change
- It's national "Phufkel" week (Create one!)

Here are some examples, with clients who have been mentioned earlier, of the surprising results you can get when you do something you are convinced no one will pay any attention to, but are determined to make the effort anyway because you never know. (Oh, and that cliché about something is so good it speaks for itself? The real truth is that nothing speaks for itself, which is why it is up to you to get the message out.)

A 50TH ANNIVERSARY

When we wrote the brochure for Rapid Park, we realized that they were soon to celebrate their 50th anniversary. The first question was to decide how important the 50th anniversary of a small family-owned collection of garages was in the scheme of things, particularly in busy Manhattan.

We could have taken the easy way out, said no one would be interested, and ignored the event. We decided we did not want to keep the news to ourselves. As I have suggested you do, we would make it seem important, and therefore it might be perceived as important. Once that was decided, my creative challenge went into attempting to create a message fitting for a parking garage company to tell the world it was their 50th anniversary. Ideally this would be a different story than if a jeweler or insurance company—or your own Phufkel company—was having a 50th anniversary. (Remember: "Whose voice is that?")

Do you have any thoughts on how a parking garage would announce its anniversary? I developed a series of small-space black and white ads similar in size and format to the regular advertising Rapid Park had been running. Here are the headlines of the ads that ran:

- ◆ 50 Years Of Keeping New Yorkers Off The Street.
- ◆ Sure You're A Good Driver. But After 50 Years, We Know How To Make You A Better Parker.
- ◆ Any Garage Can Stay Open 24 Hours. We've Been Open 50 Years.
- ◆ We Can't Teach You To Drive. But After 50 Years, We Sure Can Teach You To Park.

Because we ran the ads, did mailings with reprints, and sent out press releases, the story was indeed picked up in several relevant real estate publications.

A 70TH ANNIVERSARY

Max Asnas had opened the original Stage Deli in 1937. Now it was time to celebrate its 70th anniversary. As a legendary New York dining experience, you would think getting publicity for this event would be easy. However, there are over 20,000 restaurants in New York, each clamoring for its share of attention. Also, delis aren't fashionable or chic the way barbecue or fusion is right now, so it's not an automatic slam dunk that you can get publicity for your deli story. What you need is a good . . . oh, you knew that?

Just as I had to determine how a parking garage would announce its anniversary, the question now became how would a deli say it? More specifically, how would the Stage say it? What might catch the public's eye and the media's attention?

We needed to find an idea that was Stage specific. There was no reason to alter our basic communication strategy, which was that the Stage's reputation was based on its huge portions, celebrity sandwiches, along with a grouchy waitstaff. We had talked about saying, "Celebrating 70 Years." This certainly was clear enough, but I was not happy with it. As you undoubtedly recognize by now, an obvious concern was that anyone in any category could use that combination of words. What I did was add two words to "Celebrating 70 Years" and it became a specifically Stage Deli message. We produced a huge banner—still having to rely on good ideas, not gigantic budgets—with photos in the middle of the banner of a gigantic sandwich and a colossal cheesecake. The new headline sat on top of the pictures, "Celebrating 70 Years Of Excess."

The key, of course, was the word "excess." It was what the Stage had built its reputation on—huge portions— just said in a different, provocative manner. Two more signs continued the story. One featured a photograph of Norman Moss, an actual Stage waiter with a classic dour appearance. The words surrounding his face were "We Are All So Happy About Our 70th Anniversary . . . A Waiter Almost Smiled."

The other sign had no waiter and no cheesecake, only a picture of a huge Triple Decker sandwich with this headline: "After 70 Years, You Should Look This Good."

Events were scheduled for throughout the year, including a special limited time reduced price promotion, featuring corned beef, pastrami, and other full-sized sandwiches for just $5.95 and 50-cent egg creams. The anniversary and the special events were featured on radio, websites, and other media, including interviews with the owners. This was all done because we were convinced that the 70th anniversary was important, and treated it as such.

Good Idea: I sent a letter to the Office of the Mayor, asking to have a proclamation issued for the anniversary of this landmark institution. For the purpose of this aside, it doesn't matter if they said yes or no (Though they did say yes). Again the point is that if you treat your news as if it is important, then that will often determine how it is perceived. Request a certificate, win an award, order a plaque, then get the word out regarding your accomplishments.

Speaking of letters, here are three we sent out that had worthwhile results because we didn't allow our concern that no one would care prevent us from taking action.

THE BEST VALUE IN TIMES SQUARE

Crain's New York Business magazine ran an article saying that Applebee's was coming to Times Square and, according to the article, it would be the best value in Times Square. I truly believed that my client Dallas BBQ was, and would remain, the best value. Though I doubted *Crain's* would actually print it, I wrote a letter listing all the reasons Dallas BBQ was the best value, the client signed it, and I sent it to the Letters to the Editor section. The result? The letter was printed in *Crain's* stating the Dallas BBQ point of view under a bold heading, "Dallas BBQ. The Best Value In Times Square."

Good Idea: Read the letters to the editors in publications that are relevant to your Phufkel. Anyone say something you agree with or disagree with? (One of those two responses is likely.) Don't be shy. Send a letter to the publication stating your agreement or why you disagree with the position. If they print your response, send a copy to your mailing list (you have a database by now, don't you?). Send a copy to the author of the letter to start a dialogue that may pay off in the future.

EXPAND YOUR ENTHUSIASM

On the television show *Curb Your Enthusiasm*, the star, Larry David, had a sandwich named for him at some fictional delicatessen. He professed to be extremely unhappy with the ingredients used in his eponymous sandwich. After I saw the episode, I found out whom to contact and offered to honor Larry with a real sandwich named for him at the very real Stage Deli. We eventually received approval and a wonderful quote to use, perfectly in character for his television persona and for all I know his real life personality: "I recommend the Larry David for anyone who has no regard for their health or well-being." His sandwich went into the menu, his letter and a photograph went onto the wall, and a press release telling the story went out to the media.

DEAR MR. MAYOR

My partner Paul had an idea. He thought we should suggest to the Stage Deli that it rename its hamburger the "Mayor Bloomberger," in honor of Michael Bloomberg's expected mayoral reelection. (This was back in 2005.)

Good Idea: Just because your business card does not say "Creative Director" is no reason to shy away from developing ideas. Anyone can have a good idea. The creatives undoubtedly will get more of them, but they will also create more clinkers. Your ideas might prove even more interesting because you are not the creative director. You will be looking at the problem from a very different perspective, so you are likely to come upon a very different creative solution.

Initially I did not think the mayor would be particularly impressed with this honor. However I have learned, and occasionally remember, that I am not always right.

I wrote a letter to the mayor's office because, as this chapter's heading suggests, you never really know what will get people's attention until you try.

The letter explained that we wanted to honor his honor's expected reelection with the Mayor Bloomberger and gave examples of other celebrities who had been so honored. Then I decided to add a little irreverence as a P.S., hoping that it would help the letter stand out from the many requests the office received every day. This was the P.S.: If the unimaginable were to happen, and you were not victorious, we would still like to honor you. Of course, it would be a smaller burger, probably with no toppings, just ketchup. Maybe an onion slice. We'll see.

Good idea. On the outside of the envelope to the mayor's office, I wrote "the Stage Deli would like to name a sandwich for Mayor Bloomberg." This helped the letter to stand out even before it was opened. Think about putting something on the outside of the letters you send to make them individual. If your pithy phrase helps the recipient decide to open the letter, it has served its purpose.

What was the end result of us deciding that honoring the mayor with the Bloomberger was important and newsworthy? The mayor spent an hour at the Stage Deli on Election Day, which turns out to be one of the quieter political days of the year. The first half hour of his visit was the press coverage: TV, newspapers, and radio. The second half hour he ate lunch with the owners, chatting and enjoying his hamburger.

The encouraging thing for you should be the realization that once you decide to go ahead and spread the news it does not have to be particularly expensive. E-mails are free. The letters that were sent to *Crain's*, Larry David, and the mayor's office were just the cost of the postage. It is the good idea that makes it all work that is invaluable.

FOUR WORDS THAT WILL GUARANTEE YOUR FINANCIAL SUCCESS

Sorry.

I have no idea what those magic four words might be or if they even exist. I admit that I lured you into this chapter to make a different point.

Have you noticed that most of the many how-to, self-help, and financial guides all seem to promise to provide a unique solution to various problems and opportunities. More important, they promise to do it all with a six-word, two-sentence or at most three-step solution.

Then they write a 350-page book to explain it all to you.

If their solution is so simple and apparent, why does it take a full-size book to make the point? Okay, with a little commentary, a preface, perhaps an introduction, what are we up to? Ten pages?

When you read those books, you probably just skim them, looking for the one bit of information that will provide the answer that the title promises.

Some of you may be doing that with this book. Skipping the wonderfully insightful case histories, the cunningly crafted principles, ignoring the many invaluable good ideas sprinkled around for your benefit. All you really want is the list—the brief directive that says, "Do these things and you will quickly produce good ideas that will build your business."

You may not want to hear it, but it doesn't work that way. I never promised you five easy ways to create good ideas and build your brand.

However, I certainly understand your desire for a straightforward solution like that. So here's what I will do: This chapter will be a (very) condensed version of what I have been telling you about creating and utilizing good marketing ideas to sell more of your Phufkels.

It represents the heart of the message, guiding you with a number of "what to do's" and minimizing the "why you should's." You'll get the advice without the caveats, except for this one: It is really a good idea to read more of the book than just this summation.

- This book is *All You Need Is A Good Idea!* **NOT** *All You Need Is A Great Idea!* Spending forever trying to turn something good into something flawless will almost certainly never get you anywhere.
- At some point the creation of the idea will be the most important part of the process. But in the beginning you have to get comfortable with the method: finding the ideas, writing them down, making them as clear as possible, then making them as creative as possible.
- The first thing to do is look inside your company. Gather any marketing pieces that have been done and write down the contents as if you were copying it. This forces you to really look at and think about the words and why they flow the way they do. Next, how about speaking to your employees and your customers?
- Look outside, starting with your competitor's websites, advertising, and marketing materials. Go to your suppliers and ask them about your competition. Look for insights and viewpoints from people who have different agendas, styles, and ideas than yours.
- Knowing who you are lets you understand *what* you want to communicate; it does not tell you *how* to communicate. That's where the idea part comes in.
- You need a brief basic summation of what your product/service is, to be used as a strategic direction

for the marketing ideas you will be creating. The really good marketing ideas come directly out of your Phufkel and are not just layered on top of it.

♦ The more single-minded and unique the strategy, the more likely the ideas you generate will be compelling, persuasive, and unique. Decide who you are trying to talk to (your audience), what are you trying to tell them about your Phufkel (your message), what do you want them to do (their actions), and what reason(s) have you given them to do it (your benefits).

♦ Looking at your audience in various ways will help you define your target: It is not the quantity of people you communicate to, it is the quality.

♦ Good ideas are more than just slogans, more than a group of witty words nicely strung together. They have the strength to support a campaign and build a brand.

♦ Pulling back from something outlandish is easier than trying to convince yourself that the dull idea that has appeared in front of you is worthy of pursuing.

♦ Words and ideas that are fresh and unexpected jump off the page, as will an unexpected splash of color or an eye-catching illustration. These can help turn a tired, weak idea into a good idea.

♦ If you are lazy or just too busy or preoccupied to spend a lot of time trying to come up with an idea, please work very hard, just one time. Because once you have a good idea, the rest is reasonably easy.

♦ There is always much more you can do with your original idea. All those supplementary ways to utilize the original idea make the original struggle worth the effort.

♦ Once you have done all the preliminary thinking and have truly tried very hard to come up with a good idea, take a break. You will be surprised at what your subconscious will often come up with.

♦ Do you think you will be better off featuring one benefit or fact about your Phufkel, or do you think you will be better served having an all-encompassing multibenefit approach?

♦ What can you do to take an idea from "nice" to "good"? You must prod it, poke it, and look at it from different angles. Write down your thought in unusual ways to see if you can find that unexpected twist that makes it sing and dance.

♦ The purpose of a good idea is not to show the world how clever you can be. A good idea can be intriguing; it can't be irrelevant or puzzling. At the very least your communication should be straightforward and convey what you intend to communicate.

♦ The fewer words you can use to convey your idea, the better. Brevity is the soul of many a good idea. Your aim is to pique the reader's interest, not bring it to an end. There is a place for long copy, but unless you are a really excellent writer it is extremely difficult to do well.

♦ It is easy to attract attention with a graphic or provocative combination of words, but you must combine your shock with relevance.

♦ Avoid safe, familiar, lackluster words. If you think you have heard it before, you have.

♦ If you don't have a sense of humor, acquire one. Humor relies on a different way of looking at things, a juxtaposition that is unexpected but comes naturally out of the set up. Just as you should be doing with your communications.

♦ If your Phufkel now does its job faster, easier, more economically, less noisily, with a feature never offered before, don't merely tell your customers, show them. A visualization or demonstration of a unique quality or improvement is worth many words.

♦ If your Phufkel were a person, who would it be? When you come up with an answer, you will better understand how to present its character, temperament, attitude, and personality.

♦ When you are about to produce your good idea you will have doubts and misgivings. Bounce it off someone who has not seen it before, but be careful. If you ask enough people their opinion of a headline, and each person only changes one of the words, it is like being pecked to death by ducks.

♦ Mail, fax, or e-mail that press release. Believe it to be newsworthy and others may start to share your enthusiasm. Newspapers often need filler items, and what is small filler to them might be very significant for your business.

♦ If you really do not have earthshaking news, put a fresh coat of paint on the news you do have. Any milestone will do: It's your business's birthday, or your company has relocated. You were made an officer of an organization, or you or your company received an award. Maybe it is national "Phufkel" week (Create one!)

♦ Laminate a copy of your ad, so it will always appear fresh. Send a copy to your clients. Send a copy to your prospects. Display a copy in your window, on your wall, or on your desk. Send a copy, with a little PR piece, to your local media outlets. Or do all of the above.

♦ You should be aware of the most traditional as well as the latest technological media as possible outlets for spreading the good word about your Phufkel: brochures, press releases, trade shows, websites, blogs, direct marketing, podcasts, sock puppets, tagging, and RSS feeds.

♦ It is never good to break the rules until you actually know the rules. There will, however, be a moment when the time is right, so trust your tummy, but be careful about being pigheaded.

♦ Without driving yourself crazy by second-guessing, think about if what you have created could benefit from a little tweak, an unexpected use of color or typeface, or phrasing or punctuation? Look again at the copy breaks, the placement of the illustration, the punctuation, the typeface, and the white space.

♦ Spell checking and correct grammar are little things, but you better be sensitive to them both. Typos will kill you. "Complimentary" and "complementary" will not always be caught by spell check, but they will certainly be caught by many of your readers.

♦ When you come up with your good ideas, do not dilly or dally. Circumstances may suddenly change, rendering your good idea worthless.

♦ There may be an idea in the actual name of your Phufkel. You can make your name distinctive by something as simple as capitalizing or enlarging a letter. Stardust as a name is different from StarDust, just as StardusT is different from either one.

♦ I am sure that there have been several times when you have developed an idea that had absolutely no relationship with your creative strategy, but you said, "Oh, just this once." It comes down to this: How many times have you said, "Just this once"?

While it is helpful to read this condensed list of suggestions, you will get a lot more out of the book by beginning at the beginning.

20

HOW DID *YOU* DO?

Lawyers never ask a witness on the stand a question unless they are confident that they already know the answer. So it is sort of reckless of me to ask, "How'd you do?" since one possible response to the question posed in this chapter is, "Hey, I did what you told me and it didn't work."

Though I hope that is not your response, allow me to become defensive. Maybe yours was a bad idea. Did you strategize, agonize, create, polish, shine, and develop your good idea? Okay, I believe, you. It was a good idea. But did your mailing consist of sending out just one post-card one time? Handing out just one flier? Did you run your ad once in only one publication? If that is the case, it is the equivalent of making just one new business-prospecting phone call with no follow-up. Even a truly good idea benefits from a little repetition to get noticed and acted upon. Granted, the point of a good idea is to make the initial communication as strong and noticeable as possible, but even then it usually takes more than one shot to hit your target.

Then again, perhaps you were successful. And when you put your good ideas to use, they did all that you (and I) hoped for. Realistically, how do you know how much of your success was due to your good idea anyway?

At the end of the nineteenth century, John Wanamaker, owner of the department store Wanamaker's, stated that he knew half the money he spent on advertising was wasted. He just didn't know which half.

Sometimes you just can't easily judge the success or failure of your ideas. It is not like ordering products for resale. Buy 60 widgets, mark them up, and sell them and you will know fairly accurately how well you are doing.

I remember my agency was pitching a client, who said that he had just bought a printer, and he knew what it cost and how much the ink will cost. But he said that he had no idea, if he hired us, how much of any new business he could attribute directly to our efforts. Of course, he was right. Even if we had successfully convinced him of our wonderful track record, he had no guarantee we could repeat it for his Phufkels. Or how much of his future success was due to our marketing communication efforts. He knew that you could set goals using benchmarks along the way, do research, test, and fine tune. Then, on the day of your Phufkel marketing introduction, along comes the rainy day or a heat wave. Or right before your launch, your competition drops coupons that will keep your prospective purchasers out of the buying cycle for months. Oh well. Good ideas, like life, all too often rely on chance, coincidence, and luck. Success— and failure—often comes down to just a matter of a few seconds and one or two inches. But given that good fortune seems to favor the prepared, let us do the best we can and keep those good ideas coming.

Good News! Since you made it all the way to the last chapter, you are entitled to a bonus. Granted, if I were as marketing savvy as I claimed, I would have a big sticker on the front of the book, shouting, "FREE! Bonus Chapter." (If there is such a label on the cover, you will know I lost this fight to my publisher.) My preference is to add a few more arrows to your quiver, providing more ammunition to help you in your battle to invent good ideas. So this is the hodgepodge section. Here are insights that did not comfortably fit in other chapters, but that I thought would be helpful. They will provide additional guidance and allow me to emphasize certain points.

MECHANICS ARE FINE FOR CARS

Don't be fixated by the mechanics: the formatting, specifi-
cations, and rules you are supposed to follow to get your
ideas into print or onto your blog. The important thing for
you to concentrate on is the content of your work, not the
format. You can read a book on writing press releases and
have the mechanics down cold: how to arrange a release,
why you should end the release with three centered
number signs, the advantage of keeping all the information on one page. As we all now know, it is the content, the
good idea that will make it effective, whether or not it vio-
lates the "rules," advertently or inadvertently. That is where
you should place your energy.

IT'S NOT THE PIANO THAT MAKES
THE MUSIC

Often the ideas you come up with will tend to be ideas
you write down, as opposed to ideas that you draw up.
This is simply because most of us have more quotidian
experience with words. We write letters, reports, term
papers, business plans, proposals, and strategic briefs. That
is why the caption contest that *The New Yorker* has been
running asks the readers to submit a caption for a cartoon. They do not ask the reader to create a cartoon to
go with a caption. Unless we have a real talent, we are not
artists—doodlers perhaps, but not artists. Often though,
one picture is worth many words. Unless you are being
paid by the word, that is a good thing. However, at some
point you will need art direction help. As Sabino Caputo,
an art director I worked with, phrases it and as I said in the
section heading, "It is not the piano that makes the music."

Sabino meant that just because today almost everyone
has access to web design, page layout, and photo editing

programs doesn't mean that the result will be particularly professional or engaging. I have used sophisticated page layout programs and still have never taken advantage of all the amazing features that are in them. For example, I wouldn't recognize a bezel curve or clipping path if I fell over one. But I know enough to be able to use the program to create what are known as "copywriter roughs." These are just basic layouts to show to a client to get agreement on the direction the piece should go in. You could use roughs to give an art director an indication of what you think the important elements in the communication are. Ideally you are giving them your point of view of what should be emphasized, not how it should be accomplished. And though you may learn a little by paying close attention to how an art director creates, would you want to drill your own teeth just because you have observed a dentist really carefully? It is the skill of the graphic artist that is required, not the equipment. A good art director is worth a thousand words.

Real art directors for example, will often take off their glasses or simply squint at a page they have designed. When they do this, they know what they are looking for (the density of the page, the weight of the white space, font legibility, a general feeling for the balance and tension of the page). When you squint at the page, all that will probably happen is that it will appear blurry. There is a difference!

Good Idea: When you work with an art director, make certain you both agree on what the essence of the idea actually is. That is where the emphasis should be placed in art and type. Don't allow a smaller point in the copy to become the dominant graphic, simply because it may prove easier to visualize. Also, when you are presented with layout

alternatives—you don't want to be overwhelmed, but you should see at least three—be certain that they are real choices. One layout with three minor variations in color or headline size is not particularly helpful in making a selection. Three radically different approaches are good. Finally, allow the art directors enough time to fully explain what they were thinking when they did the layouts. Sometimes they take for granted that something will be so obvious they barely mention it in their presentation. Once it is pointed out, you may get a better understanding of their reasons and choices.

BRAINSTORMING

Brainstorming is an interesting approach to generating ideas that you may want to try. It is a group method of creation, though according to Wikipedia, the jury is still out as to whether or not it is an effective technique for enhancing either the quantity or quality of ideas. But it may be worthwhile for you to attempt. (If you are a one-person department, it is difficult to brainstorm, even with a mirror and a tape recorder. To be most effective, line up five or six people.)

The most important part of brainstorming is akin to what I have heard is the most important rule of improvisation— the elimination of negatives, the idea of, "yes, and. . . ." For example, when one person says the red broom is really his wife's piano, the other improv artist never says that is ridiculous. He builds on it, using a version of "Yes, and." So he might respond, "Yes, and that explains why Gershwin was sweeping the floor."

The basic tenet of brainstorming is to never say anything negative about anyone else's ideas. Write each idea down, the crazier the better, and let everyone build on them. Never allow anyone to suggest it will never work, it is stupid, too expensive, or there is not enough time to implement it.

CUSTOMER SERVICE AS MARKETING

It is not a good idea to attract and build your business with clever marketing and then alienate your customers with adversarial customer service when they call up with a problem. This is especially true now with the existence of websites like Consumerist.com, which stands ready to report all instances of unpleasant customer treatment. Sites like these publish phone numbers and addresses of high-level management for customers to contact directly when all else is not working. (They also praise companies that go the extra step for their customers. It is a good idea to be praised rather than pilloried.)

Your customer service policy is part of your marketing communications; it strongly reflects on your brand image and reputation. How you handle customer service—in person or online—will have a powerful impact on your Phufkel's image, as surely as your ad and slogan will. Most of you will certainly agree that putting the customer first will consistently pay off. (We have a virtual sign at Porte that says, "It's easy. Do what is best for the client." It makes decisions much easier and faster.)

Lands' End puts their customer service policy into two words: "Guaranteed. Period." Others could make a similar promise in a lot more words, with a lot less impact—and probably have.

On a positive customer service note, there is the Netflix story as reported in the *New York Times*. Netflix, a company that delivers DVDs by mail, hired 200 customer service representatives for a call center in Oregon to use as a customer service initiative. In fact, Netflix eliminated e-mail-based customer service completely. Their live customer service headquarters is open 24 hours, and its toll-free number is now prominently displayed on their web site. Michael Osier, vice president for information technology operations and customer service, said that he looked at two other companies with reputations for superb phone-based customer service and saw that customers preferred human interaction over e-mail messages.

I am not suggesting that you eliminate e-mail dialogues with your customers or stop outsourcing and/or outshoring your customer service centers, if that is what you have and what you do. Perhaps the simplest good idea for you is to think about how you feel when, as a consumer, you have to call up tech support. When you realize how often it leaves a bad taste, a feeling that often translates into a promise to never deal with that company again, you may get all the insight you need into how to handle your own customer services.

 Good Idea: Customer service doesn't begin and end with outside call centers. How is a call answered in your company? Is it done quickly, politely, and efficiently? Does upper management ever answer its own phone calls? Are calls returned promptly? The same is true for e-mail or any correspondence, especially letters of complaint.

THINK BIG (AND THINK LITTLE)

One of the ways you might be shortchanging yourself is settling for minor victories while ignoring the big picture.

You decide to have a parade because it is your company's anniversary and you want to get some publicity. Good idea. But what is your idea of a parade? One car? Two cars and a horse and wagon? Consider using equipment as big as your ideas and your budget will allow. The more cars, people, wagons, fire department trucks, and whatever else you can think of, the better. The larger the spectacle, the more likely you are to get the publicity you are seeking. In fact, the bigger the event, the more likely you are to get cooperation from the authorities to allow you to hold the parade in the first place. Can you imagine asking the police department in New York to block traffic on the FDR drive because you want to set off three flares? They would laugh at you. But when Macy's makes the same request for their big Fourth of July fireworks spectacular, the drive is closed for hours.

Speaking of Macy's, their annual Thanksgiving Day Parade certainly attracts huge crowds, live and on television. If you think your parade could never be as big, you are right. But if you think your parade *could* be as big, that is something to aspire to. It might not happen the first year, events take time to catch the public's eye. But I bet each year it will get bigger and better.

While you are thinking your grandiose plans, don't overlook the small things. In this high-tech, YouTube, RSS world, how about doing some buttons for your Phufkel? You know, those round metal things with words and a picture on the front and a pin on the back. People have worn them for years, but because they are seen less frequently now they may have more of a chance to stand out. The point is that the size of the medium doesn't matter. From an advertising slide on a local movie theater screen to neon-lighted moving spectaculars in Times Square, it is the concept, the good idea, that matters.

Marketing is still not a perfect science; heck, science is not a perfect science. And often the creative component is one you simply have to initially take on some degree of trust and give it a chance to perform. You can measure the results, thanks to hindsight, but you can't always accurately calculate the reasons why you had the huge outcome you had.

DON'T BE A STRANGER

ideas@allyouneedisagoodidea.com is where you can contact me to share particulars of your successes, details on the good ideas you have created, how you did with the blank page, your own case histories, and also provide some feedback. Or visit www.allyouneedisagoodidea.typepad.com, where you'll find the most current information on how to create marketing ideas that actually get results!

21

HOW DID *I* DO?

It occurs to me that you might be curious about what I planned on doing—and what I actually did—to market *All You Need Is A Good Idea!* After all, I have written and you have just read a book that attempts to teach you how to create marketing ideas that actually get results. What good ideas did I come up with? What ordinary or unusual, expected or unexpected marketing ideas did I utilize to make my book stand out from the 50,000 printed each year? Most important, did any of them work?

So I am going to share with you the marketing ideas I plan on using; some will work better than others, some will not pan out at all. And there will be some I have not even thought of yet that I will create and use in the future. What I mean by that—hold on tight—is that I am writing this book now, but you will be reading it in the future, which will be your present. Though this sounds a lot like an episode of *The Twilight Zone,* think of it this way: After I submit my manuscript for this book to my publisher, it will take many months before it is printed and available to you. During that time the marketing ideas I plan on using to get you to purchase this book will already have been attempted, successfully or not. If *All You Need Is A Good Idea!* is successful, then my marketing efforts have paid off and you have learned about this book from my interviews on television and radio, my blog, articles in your local newspapers, or mentions in national and business-oriented magazines. If that's the case, then you can have confidence that I do indeed have some ability in creating good marketing ideas.

Conversely, if you have stumbled across this book in a suburban garage sale, beneath the pile of 1939 *Life* magazines, and thought, "Sounds interesting, wonder why I have never heard of it," then it did not work out as well as I had hoped.

Bestseller or not, there is still value in seeing the kinds of ideas that I am thinking of to get attention for the book; perhaps some of them will trigger ideas for promoting your Phufkel, particularly if you are in the service area or writing a book of your own. Remember, it is not the quantity of the ideas; I will probably be more prolific than you will be since I create ideas for a living. And I do have the resources of my New York ad agency to call upon. Also, my publisher will be involved with marketing and public relations using their expertise and perspective; the intention is not to duplicate, but reinforce that effort.

Finally, the lists of ideas I have here will most probably not be the ones you would use. It is similar to when my agency pitches a new client. When we present the creative we have done for our current and past clients, we always make a point to say that there is no idea they will see that is right for them. Their business is different, their strategy is different, their budget is different, their Phufkel is different, and their corporate culture is different.

The point of showing prospective clients past work is to show them how we approach problems. We do not necessarily expect the prospective client to like the creative answers other clients have embraced; we do hope they relate to our thinking. So even if this is not the list you would make, it has value in showing you how I approached the marketing of *All You Need Is A Good Idea!* Your contacts, your list, your particular knowledge will make your list different, but mine may lead you into additional directions.

Some of the ideas are truly local in nature, with not much chance of a profitable payback for the time invested. But there is also a publicity aspect that is not strictly monetary; every sign in a window with my book's title will have an additive effect to building the brand.

TRADITIONAL PROMOTIONS

- ◆ Seminars
- ◆ Contact customer relations departments of bookstore chains—and local bookstores—for book signings and discussions.
- ◆ Low-tech, old-fashioned promotional items like buttons and stickies could be given out at various events.
- ◆ On a more high-tech front, I plan on using blogs, podcasts, and a website.
- ◆ Teaser/small space ads, each with a different chapter heading, book cover, and web address, might be affordable.
- ◆ Solicit mentions, reviews, and articles in national business publications; articles and interviews in national trade publications; radio station interviews; appearances on television shows, national and cable; promote the book through book clubs and direct mail campaigns; create a series of press releases to distribute to key media.

NONTRADITIONAL PROMOTIONS

- ◆ Prepublication, chief executives, and heads of marketing departments will be invited to submit what they consider their own best marketing idea. This could be the basis for a series of articles.

THE BLANK PAGE CONTEST

In the book I left one page blank, and made the point that there is very little as intimidating as staring at that blank page knowing it is up to you to fill it with a good idea. We will invite readers like you to use the blank page from the book and submit the good marketing idea they developed to my website.

On my blog I will create an imaginary product and provide details for a creative brief. For example: "Tango is a new breakfast cereal that is designed to have orange juice added to it, rather than milk. That's because new Tango. . . ." Then I will solicit visitors to the blog to e-mail their ideas for promoting this product, critique some of the better entries and award a prize.

MEDIA COVERAGE

I intend to seek coverage, reviews, and interviews in appropriate publications, such as (partial list):

♦ General Business Publications: *Barrons, Businessweek Small Business, Fast Company, Forbes, Fortune, FSB: Fortune Small Business, INC, Opportunity World, Small Business Opportunities, Start Your Own Business, Womensbiz.us, Wall Street Journal, New York Times,* and *USA Today.*

♦ Marketing Publications: *Advertising Age, The Advertiser, Adweek, Creativity, One, Brandweek,* and *Sales & Marketing Management.*

♦ Websites: Business Week: SmallBiz, http://www .businessweek.com/smallbiz/index.html; Entrepre neur.Com: The Online Small Business Authority, http://www.entrepreneurmag.com; Edward Lowe Peerspectives, http://peerspectives.org; Entrepreneur's Reference Guide to Small Business Information, http://www.loc.gov/rr/business/guide/guide2/; Fambiz.Com, http://fambiz.com; Idea Cafe: The Small Business Channel, http://www.businessowners ideacafe.com; Online Women's Business Center, http://

www.onlinewbc.gov; Patent Café, http://www.pat
entcafe.com; The Riley Guide: Steps in Starting Your
Own Business, http://www.rileyguide.com/steps.html.

♦ Marketing Associations: American Marketing
Association, Business Marketing Association,
U.S. Chamber of Commerce, U.S. Small Business
Association.

♦ Media Interviews (Partial):The Big Idea with
Donny Deutsch, CNBC; Joan Hamburg, WOR-
AM Radio 710; Stuart Elliott, advertising columnist,
the *New York Times* (fortunately we both come from
Brooklyn); Barbara Lippert, *Adweek*; Bob Garfield,
Advertising Age; the advertising/marketing columnists
at the *New York Sun*; *New York Post*; *Daily News*; and
the *Wall Street Journal*.

Newspaper Contacts

There should be an interest in *All You Need Is A Good Idea!*
in most newspapers. The business of advertising/market
ing has an appeal far beyond those actually in the business. The *New York Times* for instance has a daily advertising
column, not a daily accounting or dentistry column.

Networking

I belong to a networking group that in Manhattan alone
has more than 600 members. At the most micro level,
I can talk about my book at my weekly meetings and as a
guest at the other chapters in New York.

Contact marketing departments of universities to
determine interest in *All You Need Is A Good Idea!* as a

textbook. Perhaps speak as a guest, give seminars, or teach a marketing class.

There you have it. But though my list is written in paper, it is not written in stone. As I reflect on them, some of the marketing and promotional ideas I listed I will not even attempt. However, they will probably lead me to other good ideas (that's just the way it always seems to happen).

INDEX